Field Guide to
MUSHROOMS

Based on
Field Book of Common Mushrooms
by William S. Thomas

Revised, updated, and with
illustrations and photographs by
Marie F. Heerkens

A MAIN STREET BOOK

This field guide is not intended as an authoritative source of information on the edibility of wild mushrooms. Those wanting this knowledge should seek more information by joining a local club or society, reading many field guides, and consulting with local experts on the identification of any species found. Neither the publisher, editor, nor the reviser are in any way responsible for mistaken identifications and /or the consumption of any toxic or deadly species that may occur to anyone who fails to read or heed this warning, or those given throughout the text.

Text for this book was adapted and updated from
Field Book of Common Mushrooms
© 1928 by William Sturgis Thomas

Every effort has been made to trace the holder of the copyright. If rights have been inadvertantly infringed upon, Sterling asks that the omission be excused and agrees to make necessary adjustments in subsequent editions.

Photography and Illustrations by
Marie F. Heerkens

Editor: Cassia B. Farkas
Design and production: Alan Barnett, Inc.

10 9 8 7 6 5 4 3 2 1

Library of Congress Cataloging-in-Publication Data available upon request

© 2003 by Marie F. Heerkens
Published by Sterling Publishing Co., Inc.
387 Park Avenue South, New York, NY 10016
Distributed in Canada by Sterling Publishing
c/o Canadian Manda Group, One Atlantic Avenue, Suite 105
Toronto, Ontario, Canada M6K 3E7
Distributed in Great Britain by Chrysalis Books
64 Brewery Road, London N7 9NT, England
Distributed in Australia by Capricorn Link (Australia) Pty. Ltd.
P.O. Box 704, Windsor, NSW 2756, Australia

Manufactured in China
All rights reserved

Sterling ISBN 1-4027-0696-0

CONTENTS

Preface

by Jacqueline B. Glasthal

There are, by most estimates, more than one and a half million species of Fungi on Earth. Over 30,000 of those are mushrooms, and the more that is learned about them, the more complex the systems of classifying them become. Until 1969, for example (over 20 years after the last edition of this book was issued), scientists lumped mushrooms, molds, and yeasts with members of the Plant Kingdom. Now they are universally accepted as Fungi—a separate and distinct Kingdom in which are grouped species that, unlike plants, contain no chlorophyll, and thus are unable to produce their own food.

Of course, today's scientists have much more powerful microscopes, electron-scanning equipment, and a fine-tuned knowledge of DNA research at their disposal to help them in their close analysis of mushrooms. It is no wonder then that the classification systems used today are quite different from those of which Dr. William Sturgis Thomas (1871–1941) was aware when he created his own classification system for the first edition of this field guide.

By profession, Dr. Thomas was a physician and surgeon, and served for a time as director of the Department of Allergy at New York's St. Luke's Hospital. But as an amateur mycologist, he had a layperson's wide-eyed wonder and enthusiasm, as well as an appreciation for the importance of simplicity when imparting information. Though largely self-taught, it is notable that Dr. Thomas' knowledge of mushrooms was so well developed that, in the early 1930s when the New York Mycological Society was founded, he was selected as its first president.

The goal of this modern rendition of Dr. Thomas' classic field guide, then, is to honor and retain Dr. Thomas' insight and knowledge—yet at the same time, inform it with the most up-to-date information available in the field of mycology today. Much of Dr. Thomas' knowledge and astute observations about chanterelles, candy caps, orange mock oysters, and other mushrooms still stand the test of time, as do many of the quotes and bits of insight that he included from his fellow mycologists. In order to keep in line with the times, however, the currently accepted classification system and terminology needed to be imposed on the text. We also have included much more about the non-gilled mushrooms, about which Dr. Thomas had scanty information in earlier editions of this work. It appears to have been something he was working on, as later editions included more in this category, although not so many as appear here.

Since Dr. Thomas wrote, much has also been learned about the toxicity of some mushrooms, which can vary greatly from locale to locale and season to season. For safety's sake, then, as it is now known that individual responses to a particular species are not always the same, be aware that the recipes included here are meant to be more of an interesting exhibit of what was done in earlier editions than as any sort of culinary recommendation on the part of the current publisher.

Thus, the modernization of this field guide owes a great debt to those who played a part in its original creation, as well as to the editor and expert who helped it find its current form. As a member of the Rochester Area Mycological Association, Rochester, NY, consultant Marie Heerkens, coincidentally enough, was a colleague of Stephen Thomas, Dr. Thomas' son, who was also an avid mushroom lover until his death in 2002.

Given all the changes that have occurred in the field of mycology in the past half century, we hope that you will find this beautifully illustrated field guide to be as welcome an introduction to mushroom identification as did those who used it in its first edition those many years ago.

Introduction

HOW TO COLLECT AND EXAMINE MUSHROOMS

Mushrooms of one kind or another are to be found at almost every season but they occur in greatest abundance after showery weather in the months of July, August and September in Eastern North America. The seasons of abundance in Western North America are usually the winter months into the spring..

The collector will find a basket to be a good receptacle for them and different species may be kept separate from each other and uncrushed by having leaves or leafy twigs among them, or better yet, by being carried in paper or wax bags.

The mushroom is plucked entire from the ground or wood upon which it grows and special care must be taken not to cut or break the stem. Unless the whole mushroom is obtained it will be difficult or impossible to know whether the stem is provided with a volva or cup at the base, or whether its base is bulbous or hairy or attached to other stems. The dirt adhering to the stem, if there is any, is removed before the specimen is put with others into the receptacle. In collecting mushrooms for the table, the stems are cut off close to the cap.

The beginner is warned against attempting to identify a new species with but one or two specimens at hand. It is desirable to have for this purpose several specimens of varied stages of development, so that one or more of them may be cut across in order that the form of the gills and interior of the stem may be noted, while yet other caps may be needed for spore prints. It is important to keep separate from each other the specimens of the various species collected.

On arriving at home with the collected fungi, they should be spread out on a convenient surface, the collector remembering the liability of many species to decay quickly.

No single feature of any mushroom is sufficient to determine its identity or its edibility. It cannot be too often emphasized that the only certain way in which a mushroom may be identified is to know it thoroughly. Once its personality is established in the collector's mind, he will recognize it as he would the face of a friend.

There are other characters than general shape and color which distinguish mushrooms from each other. These other characters need careful scrutiny in determining the species to which a specimen belongs as is the case among many things met with in our everyday affairs. Careful attention to the especial characters and parts of mushrooms will soon familiarize one with their peculiarities and will enable him to use this guide or any text book on mushrooms intelligently. To this end the student of mushrooms will do well to make written notes of the features of gilled fungi collected by him.

Spore prints of mushrooms show the color of the spores and are sometimes indispensable before a specimen can be unmistakably identified. In many instances however, specimens can be identified by means of this key in the field or at home without waiting for the making of spore prints.

Spore prints are made by laying the mature cap from which the stem has been cut and gills downward upon a piece of paper. It is protected from draughts of air by being covered with a glass tumbler. In order to get satisfactory prints, care should be taken to have the gills in a vertical position. After a few hours a print of the gills, radiating from the center like the spokes of a wheel, will be found upon the paper. The color of the spore print assists in determining to what family of mushrooms the specimen belongs, each of whose spores are respectively either white, some shade of pink, rusty-brown, purple or black. Odd species vary from these standard spore colors in having lilac and green hues.

GILLED MUSHROOMS, THEIR PROPAGATION AND STRUCTURE

Gilled mushrooms, or agarics as they are called, belong to the botanical kingdom known as fungi. No leaves, flowers, pollen or seeds are to be found on any fungi.

These fungi, although rather unfamiliar to many persons, occur in profusion in one form or another, throughout the natural world. Other fungi that grow upon the higher plants, occur in endless numbers and constitute pests that damage or destroy food crops and trees. Some of them are known as rusts, others as smuts, rots, scabs and bunts. Mildews and molds also belong among the fungi as do all the yeasts with their mysterious power of bringing about the process of fermentation.

Among the fungi commonly known as mushrooms are the puffballs, club fungi, coral fungi, hedgehog fungi, truffles, gelatinous fungi, morels, stinkhorns, tube-bearing fungi

and lastly, the gilled fungi or agarics to which attention is directed in this book. All fungi, whether bacteria, yeasts or agarics, have in common an important characteristic feature that distinguishes them from the higher plants, and that is their lack of chlorophyl. This remarkable substance that makes green the leaves of trees and herbs, also enables them to utilize for their nutrition the simple elements of air, water and earth. Fungi, on the other hand, possessing no chlorophyl, must, like animals, depend for their nourishment upon living or dead organic matter. Loam, decaying wood and dead leaves support the majority of mushrooms.

Propagation of Gilled Fungi

Herbs, trees and grasses—in fact all of the higher plants are propagated from seeds that have been fertilized by contact with dust-like particles of pollen shed by a parent plant of the same species. This fertilizing contact requires for its accomplishment the union of two elements—male and female—pollen and ovum. Since mushrooms do not possess these sexual elements, so far as cross fertilization of seeds is concerned, the question arises, how are they propagated. In the case of mushrooms, the method of propagation, though more simple than it is in the case of seed bearing plants is no less wonderful. Each species of mushroom reproduces its own kind by means of very minute spores that are dropped from mature fruiting bodies and that each species can reproduce either sexually or asexually.

Single spores consist of a tiny bit of living matter or protoplasm enclosed within a wall or membrane, as an egg is contained in its shell. They are so small that one of them alone cannot be seen without the aid of a microscope but in mass they appear as dust that may have any one of several colors. Spore color affords an important means of classifying gilled fungi into groups or genera. They are exceedingly light and may be carried by the wind for long distances. They are dropped from the surfaces of the gills in vast numbers. A single mushroom of the cultivated variety commonly sold in the markets, may produce as many as one billion, eight hundred thousand spores. The shaggy-mane mushroom has been estimated to cast off five billion or more spores from a single mature fungus. The proportion of spores that reach places suitable to their development is very small; the vast majority of them are wasted.

When a cast-off spore alights on ground or decayed wood or on some other spot where conditions are favorable to its growth, it begins to germinate.

First, a tiny thread grows from it and penetrates the wood or loam upon which it rests. This thread, absorbing nourishment from organic matter in contact with it grows longer and sends out branches until a network of threads or fibres, now easily visible, is formed. This matted network of fibres or hyphæ, as they are called, is known to botanists as the mycelium or fruiting body. Those who cultivate mushrooms for the market speak of it as spawn. Weeks, months or even years, in some cases, must pass before the mycelium will grow and mature suffi-

ciently for it to be ready to develop fruit that will in turn produce fresh spores.

When the proper time has arrived, little knots or enlargements appear at one or many places on the mycelial threads. These swellings increase in size until they project outside of the soil or wood in which they started to grow. Each one of these knobs is destined to develop into a full-grown mushroom or spore-bearing structure.

The Structure and Parts of Gilled Mushrooms

A fully developed, typical gilled mushroom is rather simple in its gross structure. It is formed somewhat after the manner of an umbrella and consists of three main parts corresponding to the cover, ribs and handle. In the mushroom, these parts are known as the cap, the gills and the stem, or as botanists designate them, pileus, lamellæ and stipe.

If a gilled mushroom in the button stage of its development be cut through in the middle from top to bottom, there will be seen, in embryo, cap gills and stem, all enclosed in an outer membrane or veil. The cap is folded and its gills lie close along the stem, giving somewhat the appearance of a closed umbrella. The outer or universal veil usually disappears as the plant grows larger and as the cap expands, but in some species part of it persists throughout the life of the plant in the form of a sheath or cup enclosing the base of the stem. In other cases, part of the wrapper may be seen in the form of patches or flakes adhering to the upper surface of the mature cap. Both of these features may be seen in the fly mushroom or Amanita muscaria and they afford marks that help to identify that species.

Agarics, during the button stage of their existence are provided with another veil or membrane that extends from the stem to the margin of the cap. In some kinds of mushrooms this inner or secondary veil persists, at least in part, and by its presence aids in identification of the species possessing it. When this inner veil remains after the rupture or disappearance of the outer cover, it hides the gills from sight.

Sooner or later, during the growth of the plant, it breaks away from the edge of the cap as this expands or spreads open. In the case of most of the agarics, it disappears entirely but in some varieties, part of it remains as a collar or ring around the stem as may be seen in the common field mushroom. In still other varieties fragments of the secondary veil may be found, even in mature plants, hanging from the margin of the cap.

Let us consider some of the features possessed by mushrooms so as to know what to look for in any collected specimen that we may wish to identify.

First, it will be found that each kind has its own peculiar manner of growth; some are solitary while others grow in groups, tufts or clusters.

The place of growth of mushrooms varies within well defined limits. Some species grow only in woods, others only in open spaces and still others occur in both kinds of surroundings. Certain species grow upon wood, some upon the ground, and a few species are found on or under particular kinds of trees or in such especial places as railroad ties, manure heaps and growing moss.

Time or season of growth is a distinguishing feature of some kinds of mushrooms. In the temperate zones there are particular fungi that may be found growing during each month of the year.

Gilled mushrooms present a variety of odors which may assist in their identification, as for example in the case of the camphory lactarius with its fragrance really like that of sweet clover, or in that of the fetid russula, which smells of peach kernels. The majority of fungi possess either little or no odor or else a characteristic fungous odor that is difficult to describe.

Taste—The taste of many mushrooms when raw is mild or unnoticeable. Others are acrid and peppery to the tongue or puckery, or branny or, in some cases, nutty. Never eat the small part of the mushroom that is tasted, in case it is poisonous.

Cookery brings out odors and tastes entirely lacking in raw species.

In addition to the foregoing general characters of gilled fungi that aid in their identification are the character, color and form of their separate parts.

Cap or pileus—The cap is the part of a gilled mushroom that first attracts the collector's attention. It is covered with a skin or peel beneath which is the flesh. This flesh or trama is composed of interwoven fibres called hyphæ that can be separately seen only under the microscope.

Amongst the characters of the caps of mushrooms, there is one possessed by some varieties that is apt to confuse the inexperienced collector. When moist, these particular caps have a water-soaked or soggy appearance. When dry they lose this look and become opaque and they often become lighter in shade. Such caps are said to be hygrophanous and this feature may aid in identifying them. The rind or peel, of many species, when moist from rain or humidity, is gelatinous or sticky to the touch. These are described as being viscid.

Color—While the color of mushrooms is one of their most striking characteristics, it is not so useful a clue in all cases as the beginner in their study is apt to believe. Certain species exhibit great variability of color in different individuals. Many kinds of mushrooms resemble each other in hue so closely that they must be identified by other qualities.

Form of Cap—There is the greatest variety in the shape of the cap of gilled mushrooms. Some species have conical caps, some are bell-shaped, others flat and yet others funnel-shaped. The cap of the majority of species is convex when it is young. As the plant matures the cap usually expands and becomes flat or even depressed at the center. The edge may be regular, lobed or wavy. The surface may be smooth, dry, sticky or perhaps covered with scales.

If the cap has a knob protruding from its center it is said to be umbonate (umbo—a knob). The opposite form, that of a little pit, sometimes occurs, in which case the cap is said to be umbilicate (provided with a navel).

Where no mention in this book is made of a mushroom's form, it is assumed that the cap is of a convex form when young and is plane or nearly so when mature. When refer-ence is made to the cap of a mushroom, a mature specimen is meant unless otherwise specified.

Gills—The gills (lamellæ) are thin, knife-like blades attached by their upper edge to the under surface of the cap and extending like the spokes of a wheel (or ribs of an umbrella) from the stem to the margin. They always grow with their flat surfaces vertical. Upon these gill-surfaces are formed the spores that are cast off for the purpose of propagation.

In form gills may be broad or narrow, varying with different species. An important distinction is made between gills that extend to the stem (adnexed), those that are attached broadly to it (adnate) and others that do not reach it but are said to be free. Gills that run down the stem are termed decurrent; those that are notched in their edge near the stem are known as sinuate or emarginate.

Not always are gills thin; Cantharellus mushrooms have blunt, narrow gills resembling coarse leaf-veins. Again, the free edge of the gills, instead of being knife-edged, as is usually the case, may be notched like a saw (serrate) or wavy.

The spore-bearing surface of the gills is called the hymenium, which, in some cases, extends also across the under surface of the cap between them. The hymenium is composed of microscopic elongated cells sticking out at right angles to the surface.

From the free end of many of these protrude little prongs, usually 4 in number, each bearing a spore at its tip. The main cell is called a basidium; the prongs, sterigmata.

Those pavement cells that are sterile and bear no spores are called paraphyses.

The spores may possess any one of several colors according to the genus to which the specimen belongs. Their color often determines the hue of the gills in mature plants and it affords an important clue in ascertaining to what genus the mushroom belongs.

The spores vary in size and shape in different species. They are so light that when they are cast off from the sterigmata, and they fall in obedience to the law of gravity, it is so slowly that any breath of air propels them for a long distance.

The stem is usually attached to the under surface of the cap at its center, but some kinds of mushrooms have the stem attached to their margins and others between margin and center while still others have no stems.

Stems may be long or short, thick or thin, hollow, pithy or solid. When the inner veil remains attached in part to the stem, it is called the annulus.

The following recipes and methods of cooking mushrooms appeared in Thomas' book. They are included here for interest, as more of a museum piece, than a recommendation for culinary use.

METHODS OF PREPARING THE VARIOUS SPECIES OF EDIBLE GILLED MUSHROOMS FOR EATING

Agaricus

The wild or uncultivated Agaricus campestris or field mushroom which is gathered in the open fields, will cook in less time than it takes to cook the cultivated variety (Agaricus campestris hortensis) which is to be had in the markets. The stems, cut off close to the gills may be put aside and used as flavoring for sauces or soups. Wash the mushrooms carefully, keeping the gills down; throw them into a colander until the water has drained off from them.

Stewed Field Mushrooms Allow two ounces of butter to each pound of mushrooms. Put the butter into a saucepan and when melted, but not brown, throw in the mushrooms, either whole or cut into slices; sprinkle over them a teaspoonful of salt; cover the saucepan in order to keep in the flavor and cook slowly for twenty minutes or until they are tender. Moisten a rounding tablespoonful of flour with a little cold milk; when mixed perfectly smooth add a little white pepper; stir carefully until boiling. Then take off of the stove and serve at once. Less flour is required when the mushrooms are to be served as a sauce over chicken, steak or other made dishes.

Broiled Mushrooms Select those mushrooms that are spread open, keeping the unopened ones for other styles of cooking. Cut off the stems close to the tops. Baste well with melted butter and sprinkle lightly with salt and pepper. Heat a broiler very hot, lay the caps upon it with the gills uppermost and broil over a clear fire, turning the broiler over frequently. As soon as the mushrooms are tender, which will be in about five minutes, open the broiler, remove the caps with care and place them on slices of previously prepared, well-buttered toast. Pour over the whole a sauce made of drawn butter, or hot water thickened with flour to the consistency of cream.

Mushrooms Creamed on Toast Cut off the stems and wash and dry the caps. Put them into a pan and pour over them a little melted butter, dust them with salt and pepper and cook them in a hot oven for twenty minutes. While they are cooking, toast sufficient bread to hold them; put it on a hot platter and, as soon as the mushrooms are done, cover the bread with hot milk, being careful not to use too much, as it would make the bread pasty and too soft. Dish the mushrooms on the toast, putting each of them with the skin side uppermost; pour over them the juice from the pan and serve at once.

Mushrooms in the Chafing Dish Wash and dry the mushrooms, and cut them into slices. Allow two ounces of butter for each pound of mushrooms. Put the butter into the chafing dish and when it is hot, add the mushrooms and sprinkle over them a teaspoonful of salt. Cook slowly for five minutes, stirring the mushrooms frequently; then add one gill of milk. Cover the dish, cook for three minutes longer; add the beaten yolks of two eggs and a dash of pepper and serve at once. The yolk of eggs is the most convenient form of thickening when mushrooms are cooked in the chafing dish, but they must not be cooked too hard.

Mushrooms Under the Glass Cover or "Bell" with Cream With a small biscuit cutter, cut round pieces from slices of bread. They should be about two and a half inches in diameter and about half an inch thick. Cut the stems of fresh mushrooms close to the caps; wash them and allow them to drain. Put a tablespoonful of butter into a saucepan. When hot, throw in the mushrooms, gills uppermost and cook them for a minute or two and sprinkle them with salt and pepper. Arrange the round pieces of bread, which have been slightly toasted, in the bottom of the bell-dish. Heap the mushrooms on these; put a little piece of butter in the center of each; cover over the bell, which may be either of glass, china or silver, stand them in a baking pan and then cook in an oven for twenty minutes. While these are cooking, mix a tablespoonful of butter and one of flour in a saucepan; add a half pint of milk (or a gill of milk and a gill of chicken stock) and stir until the mixture boils; then add a teaspoonful of salt and a dash of pepper. When the mushrooms have baked for twenty minutes, remove them, lift the cover, pour a little of the sauce over them, cover them again and send them at once to the table.

Cream of Mushroom Soup Wash and chop finely a half pound of mushrooms and put them into a saucepan with a tablespoonful of butter and, if you have it, a cup of chicken stock; if not, use a cupful of water. Cover the vessel and cook slowly for thirty minutes. Next, put a quart of milk into a double boiler and add to it a tablespoonful of butter and two tablespoonfuls of flour rubbed together until smooth. Stir all and cook until thick; then add the mushrooms and season to taste with salt and pepper.

Agaricus arvensis may be cooked like its close ally the common mushroom. English epicures shun it but the French people prefer it to that species as a dish.

Amanita cœsarea is edible but the reader is advised not to eat it on account of the danger of confusing other kinds that are poisonous, with it.

Amanita vaginata, though edible, is very likely to be confused with poisonous Amanitæ as the resemblance is close. Dr. Murrill's dictum should be followed in this case. He says, "edible, but eat not!"

Armillaria mellea. Authorities differ as to the edible qualities of this species. Peck considered it "a perfectly safe species, but not of the best quality." I have eaten it but do not care for it. Young and small specimens should be selected for the table. It is best when fried after having been boiled for five minutes in salted water.

Kate Sargeant gives the following directions for stewing the honey-colored mushroom: Soak the caps for half an hour in water to which vinegar has been added in the proportion of one tablespoon to the quart. Roll a tablespoonful of butter in some flour and put it in a saucepan; add the mushrooms and sufficient water to cover them; stew until the caps are tender. Season with salt and pepper and serve while hot.

Cantharellus cibarius

The chantarelle. Light and soft specimens should be discarded as they become leathery when cooked; crisp and heavy plants should be chosen for the table. All those that have been partly eaten by slugs or worms should also be rejected. If, when the chantarelles are brought into the kitchen, they are scalded in milk and are left to soak in it until the next day, they will be very tender.

Cut the chantarelles across into slices and remove the stems; put the caps into a covered saucepan with a little fresh butter and sweat them; then stew in gravy or fricassee until they are tender, at the lowest possible cooking temperature; a great heat destroys their flavor.

Another recipe. Put the prepared chantarelles into boiling water for a few minutes; then stew them in fresh butter to which has been added a little olive oil, chopped tarragon, pepper, salt and lemon peel. Allow them to simmer gently over a slow fire for twenty minutes, moistening them from time to time with a little beef gravy or cream. When about to be served, thicken the stew with yolk of egg.

A more simple dish may be made by frying the chantarelles in butter or olive oil and laying them on toasted bread, adding pepper and salt as required or they may be minced and stewed alone or with minced meat.

N.B.—The chantarelle may be prepared like the common mushroom if care is taken not to cook it too hot. If boiled too violently it will become as tough as leather.

Cantharellus aurantiacus (now known as Hygrophoropsis aurantiaca). Orange chantarelle; false chantarelle. Contradictory statements exist as to the edibility of this mushroom. I have eaten it with enjoyment and with no ill effects. Since it is under suspicion, the reader is advised to let it alone as far as eating is concerned.

Cantharellus cinnabarinus is a desirable edible species which, although of small size, often occurs in abundance. It is good either stewed or fried. The stems should be removed before cooking.

Cantharellus umbonatus. As an edible mushroom this species is not as tender as some others nor is it as highly flavored but it is satisfactory and agreeable.

Cantharellus floccosus (now known as Gomphus floccosus; can cause gastric upset). Although often growing to a rather large size, is not tough but, when cut into small pieces is easily cooked in any of the usual methods. Its quality is good.

Cantharellus minor, although not considered as equal in quality to the best mushrooms, may be cooked with other species and will help to eke out what would be a scanty mess without it.

Clitocybe multiceps (now known as Lyophyllum decastes). According to McIlvaine, should be well cooked. The addition of a little lemon juice or sherry conceals a slight raw taste that is sometimes present.

Clitocybe odora is said to be exceedingly spicy. The flavor is pleasant but rather strong. A few specimens mixed with other species of like texture but with less flavor make a tasty dish. McIlvaine.

Clitopilus abortivus (now known as Entoloma abortivum). Edible in either its undeveloped (abortive) condition or in the perfect form but is of inferior quality. I prefer it when fried, with onion.

Clitopilus prunnulus is highly praised as food by some writers. Dr. Badham recommended it stewed or fricasseed, with a sauce made as follows:

Bruise in a mortar some almonds with a little water; add salt and pepper and some lemon juice; rub the whole together until it is of the consistency of table mustard.

Collybia acervata is said to be tender, delicate and of fine flavor. It should not be cooked too long.

Collybia confluens is of good substance and flavor.

Collybia platyphylla (now known as Megacollybia platyphylla). Although edible, its taste is not especially attractive. It is a good plan to mix it with other more savory species when the collected mess happens to be scanty. Then it absorbs the taste of its companions in the dish and supplies bulk.

Collybia radicata (now known as Xerula furfuracea). One of the best tasting of mushrooms. The caps should be broiled or fried.

Collybia velutipes (now known as Flammulina velutipes). A valuable species because of its extended season and good eating quality.
• Coprinus atramentarius
• Coprinus comatus
• Coprinus micaceus

As these species are not dissimilar in texture, recipes for cooking them are alike. Being soft and juicy, they must be handled with care and are better when cooked with dry heat.

To bake: Remove the stems, wash and drain in a colander; arrange the caps in a baking pan; dot here and there with small bits of butter, allowing a tablespoonful to each half-pound of mushrooms. Dust them with salt and pepper, put them into a very hot oven and bake them for thirty minutes. Serve in a heated vegetable dish, pouring over them the sauce from the pan.

To cook Coprinus. (Mrs. Rorer.) Wash and drain in a colander. Spread out in a long baking pan; dust lightly with salt and pepper and put on them a few bits of butter. Cover with another pan and bake in a moderate oven for twenty-five minutes. Add four tablespoonfuls of cream, bring to the boiling point and dish on toast.

Coprinus micaceus; another method.
Wash and dry the mushrooms; put them into a deep saucepan with a tablespoonful of butter to each quart. Hold them over a quick fire, keeping the saucepan in motion but not stirring with a spoon for fear of breaking the caps. As soon as they have reached the boiling point, push them to the back part of the stove for five minutes and then serve on toast. They will be dark in color but are very palatable and are, perhaps, the most easily digested of all fleshy fungi.

Hygrophorus cantharellus requires long cooking. Its peculiar taste is acceptable to some persons.

Hygrophorus miniatus, in Dr. Peck's opinion, is scarcely surpassed by any mushroom in tenderness and agreeableness of flavor.

Hygrophorus pratensis requires careful cooking as it is liable to be condemned as tough unless treated slowly, but it is a great favorite, says M. C. Cooke.

Laccaria laccata (this species has toxic lookalikes in the genus Entoloma). while edible, is not especially well-flavored.

Laccaria ochropurpurea is said to lose its toughness when cooked and to make a good dish.

Lactarii. In McIlvaine's opinion the juice of the milky mushrooms and their flavor are best retained when they are baked. They become hard and granular if cooked at too high a temperature. The edible species are good eating when carefully cooked in any manner.

Lactarius camphoratus has a strong taste that may be improved by the addition to it of some specimens of other milder species.

Lactarius deliciosus (now known as Lactarius deterrimus). The flesh of this mushroom is firm, juicy and nutritious. It may be cooked in the following manner: Take sound, young specimens and cut them to a uniform size; place them in a pie dish, with salt, pepper and a little butter; tie a paper over the dish and bake gently for three-quarters of an hour. Serve them in the same hot dish.

This mushroom requires to be stewed for about forty minutes. It may be fried in considerably less time.

Lentinus lepideus. A tough species, but when the stem has been removed, the caps finely sliced and fried in butter, or stewed for thirty minutes, it is good eating. Young specimens are equal to the oyster mushroom. A good soup can be made from older specimens.

Lepiota americana. In flavor this species is not much inferior to the parasol mushroom (Lepiota procera) but when cooked in milk it imparts its own reddish color to the material in which it is cooked. Nevertheless it is a fine addition to the list of edible species. Peck.

Lepiota procera; parasol mushroom.

This is one of the best of mushrooms for preservation by drying. In this condition it is easily preserved and will add much flavor to an ordinary meat sauce.

The parasol mushroom, having thin flesh and broad gills, must be cooked quickly. Remove the stems, take the caps in your hand, gill side down, and with a soft rag wash the tops, removing the brown scales. Put them into a baking pan or on a broiler. Lightly baste them with melted butter as they lie with their gills uppermost and dust them with salt and pepper. Place the serving dish to heat. Put the mushrooms over a quick fire, skin sides down for just a moment, then turn them and broil them for an instant on the gill sides and serve them at once on the heated plate.

When cooked in this way Lepiota procera is one of the most delicious of all mushrooms but if cooked in moist heat it becomes tough and unpalatable. If baked too long, it becomes dry and leathery. It must be cooked quickly and eaten at once. All the edible lepiota may be cooked in this manner.

Lepiota procera omelette. Mince some young, fresh caps; season them with pepper and salt, add butter and set them in the oven while you beat well the whites and yolks of

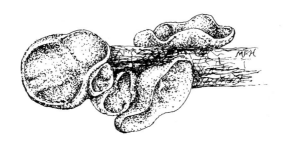

six eggs. Then put two ounces of butter into the frying pan and heat it until it begins to turn brown. Having again beaten the eggs, add three tablespoonfuls of the mushrooms and a little milk. Pour all into the boiling butter; stir in one direction and fry on one side for only five or six minutes; drain the fat off, fold the omelette on itself and serve quickly on a hot, covered dish. Kate Sargeant.

Marasmius oreades has long been esteemed as edible but owing to its small size and somewhat tough substance it has not gained the general popularity that it deserves. The following recorded opinions of it may be of interest:
- It is very good and may be eaten in an omelette.
- It has a very agreeable taste and odor and gives a delicious flavor to sauces but it needs long cooking.
- It is delicious when broiled with butter.
- It may be pickled or dried for future use.
- Its tendency to toughness may be overcome by proper cooking.

An esteemed correspondent gives the following method of cooking this mushroom:

Throw the clean caps into sufficient boiling water to make a nice gravy when done and cook them for half an hour. Then rub together a small quantity of butter, flour and water with salt and pepper and add them to the mushrooms, stirring for a moment. Pour on hot toast and serve on a hot dish.

Another method is to put the caps in water with butter and seasoning and let them simmer slowly for ten or fifteen minutes. Then thicken with flour and serve alone or pour over cooked meat.

As a condiment, chop the caps into small pieces and add them to cooking hash, stews,

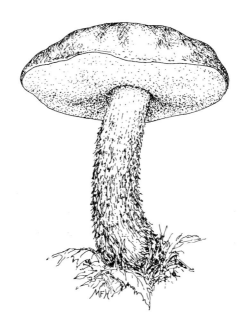

broths or meats just before the time of serving them. Peck.

Marasmius oreades pickles. Collect fresh young caps of the fairy-ring mushroom and cut the stems quite close and throw the caps into a basin of salted water. Drain them and lay them on a soft cloth to dry. For each quart of mushrooms take nearly a quart of pale white wine vinegar and add to it a heaping teaspoonful of salt, half an ounce of whole peppers, an ounce of bruised ginger, two large blades of mace and one-quarter of a teaspoonful of cayenne pepper tied in a piece of muslin. When this liquid is boiling, throw in the mushrooms and boil them in it for from six to nine minutes. When the caps have become tolerably tender put them into warm, wide-mouthed bottles, dividing the spices equally among them. When cold cork well and stand in a dry place where they will not freeze.

Panus strigosus, when mature, is of woody texture but when specimens are young, they may be used for making soup.

Pholiota adiposa (now known as Pholiota aurivella) is not classed as edible by European authorities but Dr. Peck found its flavor agreeable and its substance digestible and harmless. It is well to peel the caps before cooking them.
• Pleurotus ostreatus
• Pleurotus sapidus
• Pleurotus ulmarius

To make soup, clean the caps, cut them into small pieces and stew them until they are tender, seasoning with butter, salt and pepper; then strain. Mushrooms that are too tough to be eaten may be used in this way. The clear broth is delicious; but if one prefers, milk or still better, cream may be added.

Pleurotus sauce. A desirable addition to any meat stew may be made by chopping up young, tender caps of the oyster mushroom and stewing them in the meat stock with salt and pepper. This is poured over the veal or other meat.

Stewed. Wash and dry the Pleuroti and cut them into strips crosswise with the gills, trimming off all the tough portion near the stems. Put the mushrooms into a saucepan, adding a tablespoonful of butter to each pint of them. Sprinkle lightly with salt, cover and cook slowly for twenty minutes. Moisten a tablespoonful of flour in a half-cup of milk and when this is smooth, add another half-cup; pour this into the mushroom mixture; add a little grated nutmeg, a few drops of onion juice and a dash of pepper as it comes to the boiling point. Remove the pan from the fire and serve as you would if the dish were of stewed oysters.

Mock oysters. Cut the caps into pieces of the size and shape of oysters. Dip each into the beaten yolk of an egg to which a tablespoonful of water has been added; roll them i n cracker crumbs or corn-meal; season with salt and pepper and fry in smoking hot fat, butter or olive oil, as oysters are treated, and serve at once.

Oyster mushrooms with cheese— au gratin. Cut the washed caps into medium-sized pieces. Stew slowly, rather dry, for fifteen minutes. Pour off the liquor and save it for use later. Place the caps in a baking dish (or in individual dishes or clam-shells) in a layer, buttering and seasoning it. Sprinkle this layer with breadcrumbs and grated cheese. On this layer place another similar one and repeat until this dish is filled and has a layer of grated cheese on its top. Pour the saved liquor over the whole. Place the dish in a slow oven and bake until the top is well browned.

This manner of cooking is a favorite. Any mushroom may be cooked in this manner. McIlvaine.

Pluteus cervinus. The caps only, are tender. The stems are much tougher than the caps and hence they should not be cooked together. The caps may be cooked as described under "General recipes." The stems, when fried in butter or broiled, are very good eating. McIlvaine.

Russula. The edible members of this genus may all be cooked after the same recipes. After removing the stems and washing and draining them, they may be broiled or baked. They are also attractive when chopped into small pieces and served with mayonnaise dressing or stuffed into peeled tomatoes or with the same dressing on lettuce leaves.

While russulas apparently do not contain less water than do other species, their flesh is rather dense and they do not so quickly melt upon being exposed to heat.

The green russula (Russula virescens) may be cut into thin slices, mixed with the leaves of water cress, covered with French dressing and served on slices of tomato. It is well to peel mushrooms when they are to be served raw.

Russula fried with bacon. Fry crisp four thin slices of bacon and lay them on a platter, then fry in the bacon fat a quart of russulas, carefully selected; salt and pepper them and fry them until they are tender. Serve on the platter with bacon.

Russula delica (now known as Russula brevipes). Peck remarks that this species is excellent when fried in butter.

Tricholoma equestre (also known as Tricholoma flavovirens). This species is excellent when fried; also when creamed and served as patties. When cooked as a soup with water, pepper and salt, it resembles turkey broth. After straining—the soup should be clear—a small amount of butter should be added.

Tricholoma personatum (now known as Lepista nuda or Clitocybe nuda).

To bake. Cleanse and peel the caps, cut off the stems and lay the mushrooms, gills up, upon a baking dish; prepare a stuffing of chicken, veal or beef, fill the caps with this, cover the dish and bake for twenty minutes.

To broil. Clean and remove the stems and broil over a clear fire on both sides for a few minutes; arrange the caps on a dish over freshly made toast; sprinkle with salt and pepper, put a small piece of butter on each and set in the oven to melt the butter. Then serve quickly. Bacon cooked over the mushrooms in place of butter is thought by some to improve their flavor.

To stew. Wash the caps and cut them into small pieces. Stew them in water for thirty minutes. Pour off the water and add milk, slightly thickened with flour, seasoning with pepper, salt and a little chopped parsley. Heat and serve.

THE SPECIES

The genus *Agaricus* includes only such brown spored species as have their gills free from the stem with a ring or collar upon the stem. All of them grow upon the ground only.

Agaricus arvensis
► **Horse Mushroom**

"The horse mushroom, also called meadow mushroom, is so much like the common mushroom that some botanists have supposed it to be a mere variety of that species. The most notable differences are its larger size, its hollow, somewhat bulbous stem, its peculiar veil or collar and the paler gills of the young plant. The cap in dried specimens is apt to assume a yellow color which does not pertain to the common mushroom." Charles H. Peck.

The cap is smooth, or slightly flocculent (with a few flakes upon its surface); white or yellowish; 2 to 5 inches broad.

Gills are at first whitish or very slightly pinkish, turning dull pink, then blackish brown. They are close together but free from the stem.

The stem is white, stout, hollow, somewhat thicker or bulbous at the base, the upper part membranous, the lower part thicker. It is 2 to 4 inches long and has a yellowish double ring, split radially.

Spores brown; elliptic; .0003 to .0004 inch long.

Above right: *A group of* Agaricus arvensis *in various stages of growth from button to maturity.* **Below right:** *This detailed view of* Agaricus arvensis *shows the thick ring and young pinkish gills.*

COMMON NAME Horse Mushroom

SEASON July–September

EDIBILITY Edible

LOCATION Found on the ground in cultivated fields, grassy pastures and waste places. It is occasionally found under trees and even within the borders of thin woods, scattered or in groups

Agaricus
Genus

Agaricus campestris
► Common Mushroom, Meadow Mushroom

The common mushroom, sometimes called the edible mushroom, as if it were the only edible species, is perhaps more generally used and better known than any other.

Its dangerous look-alike is an amanita with white gills that grows from a cup-like volva, or bulbous and roughened base. The meadow mushroom should be gathered with care to be sure the gills are pink and that it is not growing from a volva.

The cap is silky or with scales; in very young plants the cap is almost globular or hemispheric and the gills are concealed (buttons). When older, the cap expands to nearly flat, and the veil separates from the margin, revealing the delicate-tinted pinkish gills. The margin, especially in young plants extends beyond the gills and is white or with dingy hues. The flesh is white or with a tendency to become pinkish when cut; taste mild and pleasant. Grows 1.50 to 3 inches wide. Gills free from stem, close together, pink when young, turning brown, then black with age; .

Stem smooth; white or whitish; short; with a ring when young; stuffed; cylindric; 2 to 3 inches long.

Spores brown; elliptic; .00025 to .0003 inch long.

Above: Agaricus campestris *is typically found growing in grassy areas, it is the closest wild relative to the cultivated button mushroom.*

COMMON NAME Common Mushroom, Meadow Mushroom

SEASON July–September

EDIBILITY Edible

LOCATION On ground in grassy places, in pastures, on lawns and manured ground, in mushroom beds, never in thick woods; singly or in groups

Family

Above: *This group of* Agaricus placomyces, *found in a mixed woods habitat, has a flattened disc on the cap.*

Agaricus placomyces
▶ **Flat-topped Agaricus**

Cap large; convex; becoming flattened with a broad raised umbo; covered with small grayish brown scales on a white background color; white flesh; 1 to 4 inches broad.

Gills at first white turning pink, then dark brown; close together; free from the stem.

Stem stout; hollow; bulbous at the base; white staining yellow on the base; ring single-layered with cottony patches on the under-surface; 1.50 to 4 inches long.

Spores brown; oval to elliptic; smooth; 4.5 to 6 x 3.5 to 4.5 microns long.

This agaricus should be avoided and has a key characteristic in that the base stains a lemon yellow; any agaricus staining bright yellow should be considered poisonous. Other look-alikes that should be avoided include *Agaricus meleagris* and *A. pocillator.*

COMMON NAME Flat-topped Agaricus

SEASON June–September

EDIBILITY Possibly poisonous

LOCATION On ground in woods, grassy areas or sawdust piles. Scattered or in groups

Above: Agaricus silvicola *grows in rich soil of the forest floor with a yellowish-tan staining stem; however the base does not stain bright yellow.*

Agaricus silvicola
▶ **Forest Mushroom**

"The forest mushroom has been regarded by some mycologists as a variety of the common mushroom, from which it is easily distinguished by its longer and hollow bulbous stem and by its place of growth (woods)." Charles H. Peck.

"It is an attractive plant because of its graceful habit and the delicate shades of yellow and white." G. F. Atkinson.

Cap convex or expanded; often with an elevation or umbo in the center; smooth or slightly silky; white or tinged with yellow or pink; the flesh whitish or tinged with pink; 2 to 5 inches broad.

Gills thin; close together; free from stem; rounded near the stem; pinkish when young, becoming darker when old; finally brown or blackish-brown.

Stem long; with a ring which is sometimes double; smooth; bulbous at base; white, often yellowish below; stuffed or hollow; 4 to 6 inches long.

Spores brown; elliptic; .0003 inch long, .00016 inch broad.

COMMON NAME Forest Mushroom

SEASON August–September

EDIBILITY Edible

LOCATION On ground in woods and groves; scattered or singly

Agrocybe
Genus

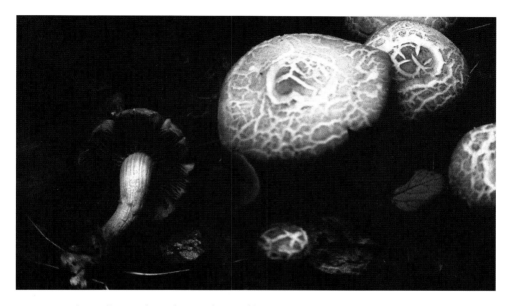

Above: *This group of* Agrocybe acericola *is one of the species that grow on wood chips in late springtime.*

The mushrooms in the genus *Agrocybe* were formerly placed in the *Pholiota* or *Naucoria* genera. Some are edible, however the edibility of the majority is unknown.

Agrocybe acericola
▶ Maple Agrocybe

One of a group of spring mushrooms that commonly grow in wood chips used for gardening, very similar to the spring *Agrocybe*

praecox, formerly known as *Pholiota praecox*, that has a more slender stem.

The cap is convex, growing to plane in age; can have central knob; ochre-yellow to brown fading to tan; sometimes moist when fresh, becoming cracked; 1 to 4 inches broad.

Gills attached; close; off-white becoming brown.

Stem white; becoming grayish-brown; persistent pendant ring striate on upper surface, often colored with brown spores; 1 to 5 inches long.

Spores cinnamon brown; elliptic, smooth; 8 to 11 microns long.

COMMON NAME Maple Agrocybe

SEASON April–September

EDIBILITY Edible, with caution

LOCATION In clusters or groups on decaying wood or wood chips in spring

Amanita
Genus

Above: Amanita phalloides *is one of the most deadly mushrooms, it was imported accidentally with European trees.*

The genus of fungi known under this name possess characteristic peculiarities of the stem. At its base is a volva or cup. The very young plants are wholly enveloped in a membrane or universal veil which is ruptured by the growth of the plant, the portion persisting at the bottom forming the above-mentioned cup or sheath. That portion of the universal veil which in the young plant covers the cap, remains in the mature plants of some of the species in the form of patches or warts, often easily separable. It sometimes happens that these warts are washed off by the rain. The gills are free from the stem which is furnished with a membranous collar or ring. The plants are generally large and attractive in appearance. Inasmuch as our most dangerous species belong to this genus the amateur should avoid eating all mushrooms having stems with a cup at the bottom or with a ring upon the stem in combination with any suspicion of a cup at the bottom.

Amanita phalloides
▶ **Poison Amanita, Death Cap, Deadly Amanita**

The Poison Amanita has a sort of deceptive character about it. It is very variable in the color of the cap and is very neat and attractive

COMMON NAME Poison Amanita, Death Cap, Deadly Amanita

SEASON July–October

EDIBILITY Deadly poisonous

LOCATION Found on the ground in woods, groves, open places and bushy pastures

Family

in its appearance and "looks as if it might be good enough to eat." This appearance is fortified by the absence of any decidedly unpleasant odor or taste, but let anyone who would eat it beware, for probably there is not a more poisonous or dangerous species in our mycological flora. To eat it is to invite death.

"I found several of this species in a lawn distant from the woods. This should cause . . . those not thoroughly familiar with the appearance of the plant to be extremely cautious against eating mushrooms simply because they were not collected in or near the woods. The bulb of the deadly amanita is usually inserted quite deep in the soil or leaf-mold, and specimens are often picked leaving the very important character of the *volva* in the ground, and then the plant might easily be taken for the common mushroom, or more likely for the smooth *Lepiota naucina*, which is entirely white, the gills only in age showing a faint pink tinge. It is very important, therefore, that until one has such familiarity with these plants that they are easily recognized in the absence of some of these characters, the stem should be carefully dug from the soil." G. F. Atkinson.

According to Charles H. Peck, "The differences between *Amanita phalloides* and the common mushroom are these:

Poison Amanita: Gills persistently white; stem equal to or longer than the diameter of the cap with a broad distinct bulb at the base.

Common Mushroom: Gills pink, becoming blackish-brown; stem shorter than the diameter of the cap, with no bulb at the base."

Amanita phalloides is not native to the Americas. Being a *mycorrhizal* species, it was unintentionally imported with European trees and is spreading. This species causes the majority of mushroom poisonings, especially among immigrants familiar with look-alike, edible species in their native country that grow from a cup at the base of the mushroom.

The cap is bell-shaped or almost globular when young, becoming nearly plane when mature. The surface is slightly viscid (sticky) when fresh and moist, and can be smooth or decorated with scattered warty patches. The margin is rarely striated. Its smooth flesh is extremely poisonous but not objectionable to the taste, although it sometimes has a disagreeable odor. It varies in color from pure white to yellow, yellowish-green, smoky-olive, gray, brown or blackish. 1.5 to 5 inches broad. (A pure white cap is *A. verna* or *A. virosa*.) The gills are white, free from, but sometimes pressed against, the broad stem. The stem is usually white and is sharply bulbous at the base. It has a wide ring near the upper end, and a *volva*, or cup, at the bottom and can be smooth or slightly scaly, stuffed or hollow, 2.5 to 6 inches long. The spores are 7 to 10 microns in diameter, white, smooth, globular, and hyaline (glassy).

Above: *This group of* Amanita virosa, *a deadly poisonous mushroom, was found growing on a lawn; it typically is found on the ground in the woods.*

Amanita virosa
▶ **Destroying Angel**

Also called Poison or Deadly Amanita. One of the most deadly mushrooms and also one of the most beautiful, with its satiny-white contrast against brown leaves or grass. Of a group with similar white Amanitas, known as *Amanita verna, A. bisporigera,* and *A. ocreata,* all of which are deadly poisonous.. It can mimic an edible *Agaricus* when in its young, unexpanded form, or even look like a small puffball. However, it can be identified by looking for the cuplike volva and making a cross section to reveal the immature mushroom outlined within.

Cap satiny white, convex to flat, swelling in center; smooth, tacky when moist; flesh white; without striations; 1 to 5 inches wide.

Gills white; free or slightly attached; close; narrow to almost broad in width.

Stem white; sometimes shaggy with torn hanging ring and a bulbous base in a cup-like volva; 2 to 8 inches long, 0.25 to 0.75 inch thick. Spores white; round; smooth; 9 to 11 microns long, 7 to 9 microns wide.

COMMON NAME Poison Amanita, Destroying Angel, Deadly Amanita

SEASON July–November

EDIBILITY Deadly poisonous

LOCATION On ground, in woods or grassy places near trees

Amanita brunnescens v. brunnescens
▶ **Cleft-foot Amanita**

Cap egg-shaped at first, then convex and later expanded; surface with whitish patches; brown to olive brown, staining reddish-brown when bruised; margin smooth; flesh white, changing to reddish-brown when bruised; 2 to 6 inches broad.

Gills free from stem; close together; white.

Stem with a ring or collar upon its upper portion; bulbous at the base with usually four characteristic splits; whitish, but generally with brownish stains especially near the base; stuffed; 2 to 6 inches long.

Spores white; ellipsoid; smooth; glassy (hyaline); 7.8 to 9.4 x 7.5 to 8.5 microns in diameter. Sometimes with a raw potato odor. The similar *Amanita brunnescens v. pallida* has a white to light yellow cap and a stronger odor of potatoes.

Above: *This specimen of* Amanita brunnescens v. brunnescens *shows the large distinctive bulbous base, reddish-brown coloring on a white stem and a red-brown cap with bright white scales.*

COMMON NAME Cleft-foot Amanita

SEASON July–October

EDIBILITY Possibly poisonous

LOCATION Found commonly in woods and groves on ground

Amanita cæsarea
▶ **Orange Amanita**

Also called Cæsar's Mushroom or Royal Agaric. The species is not generally common in America but is described on account of its importance and beauty. Occasionally groups of this mushroom can be found in the same locality each year.

"The fly amanita (*Amanita muscaria*) resembles this mushroom in size, shape and color of the cap, but in other respects they are quite distinct.

The chief distinctive characteristics may be contrasted as follows:

Fly amanita; Cap warty, gills white, stem white or slightly yellowish.

Orange amanita; Cap smooth, gills yellow, stem yellow." Charles H. Peck.

Cap orange or red, fading on the margin; smooth except at the margin where it is furrowed or striate; bell-shaped, becoming expanded when old and then the surface may be nearly flat or the center elevated; 3 to 6 inches broad; flesh white or tinged with yellow.

Gills yellow; free from stem.

Stem yellow; with a broad yellowish ring hanging like a broad collar from the upper part; is slightly bulbous at the base where it is covered by the large sac-like white volva or cup; hollow or stuffed; 4 to 6 inches long; 0.50 inch or more in thickness.

Spores white; elliptical; .0003 to .0004 inch long.

The colors of the plant are generally deeper in large specimens.

Opposite: *A group of* Amanita caesarea *shows that the brilliant color in the young "egg" stage (left) continues into maturity on the expanded caps.* **Below right:** *The egg-shaped young* Amanita caesarea *expand to reveal distinctive yellow gills and stem.*

COMMON NAME Cæsar's Mushroom, Orange Amanita, Royal Agaric

SEASON July–September

EDIBILITY Edible, but eat not

LOCATION On ground, in woods; scattered

Amanita
Genus

Amanita fulva
▶ Tawny grisette

This mushroom was formerly known as
Amanitopsis vaginata v. fulva. It does have
some toxic to deadly look-alikes and is not
recommended as an edible mushroom.

"The sheath or wrapper at the base of the
stem adheres so slightly to the stem that if the
plant is carelessly pulled the sheath is left in
the ground. My own experience indicates that
it is a fairly good mushroom, but there are
many others that I like better." Charles H. Peck

"The variations in color presented by this
species are often very bewildering to the
beginner." Murrill

Cap rather thin; smooth or adorned when
young with a few adherent fragments of the
veil (warty); bell-shaped to expanded; sometimes umbonate; deeply (striated) furrowed
at the margin; regular in form but fragile and
easily broken; reddish-brown but exceedingly
variable in color. 2 to 4 inches wide.

Gills free from stem; white or whitish to
cream; close; fragile.

Stem without a ring but sheathed at the
base by the torn remains of the rather long,
thin, flabby volva (veil or wrapper); smooth
or adorned with minute scales; variable in
color; hollow or stuffed; portions of the conspicuous white volva are sometimes carried
up as patches on the cap. 3 to 5 inches long.

Spores white; round; smooth; glassy
(hyaline); 8 to 10 microns in diameter.

Above: *These specimens of* Amanita fulva, *commonly known
as the "Tawny Grisette," do not have a ring.* **Right:** Amanita
fulva *is found in mixed woods and was considered a color form
of* Amanita vaginata.

COMMON NAME Tawny grisette

SEASON June–October

EDIBILITY Edible, but eat not

LOCATION On ground or very decayed
wood; singly or scattered in woods and
open places

Family

Amanita muscaria v. formosa
▶ **Fly Amanita, Fly Agaric, False Orange, Fly Poison**

"The fly amanita is one of our most common poisonous species. It is also very variable in color and in the size of its cap. It is generally a most showy and attractive plant. I have seen a single cap surrounded by a circle of lifeless flies that had sipped the viscid juice from its moist surface and fallen victims to its virulent properties before leaving the place of their fatal repast.... Some of the people of northern Asia make an intoxicating liquor of this fungus by steeping it in water." Charles A. Peck.

"Infusions of it are used as a fly poison. It is a striking and handsome plant because of the usually brilliant coloring of the cap in contrast with the white stems and gills, and the usually white scales on the surface." G. F. Atkinson.

The poisonous properties of this fungus are due to a principle known as muscarin which is used as a medicine and the antidote to which is atropine, an alkaloid extracted from the belladonna plant.

"Cap bright red or orange when young, fading to yellow on the margin when mature; occasionally white throughout; smooth, sometimes with minute furrows or striate on margin; adorned with white or yellowish warts or scales, or smooth if these have been washed off by rain; flesh white or yellowish just under the skin or peel; 3 to 8 inches broad; slightly viscid when fresh." Dr. W. A. Murrill.

Gills white; free from stem; rarely tinged with yellow.

Stem furnished with a collar or ring; bulbous at the base; the bulb as well as the base of the stem is scaly at times from the adhering fragments of the wrapper or universal veil, the remains of which do not form such a well-defined cup or sheath as is the case in some other *amanitæ*, such as *Amanita phalloides* or *Amanita virosa*; white or slightly tinged with yellow; 4 to 6 inches long.

Spores white; broadly elliptic; .0003 to .0004 inch long.

Above right: The mature Amanita muscaria v. formosa *can have a cap that is over eight inches wide.* **Below right:** *Young* Amanita muscaria v. formosa *mushrooms have a variety of cap colors from yellow to red with a long shaggy stem buried in pine needles.*

COMMON NAME Fly Amanita, Fly Agaric, False Orange, Fly Poison

SEASON June–frost

EDIBILITY Poisonous

LOCATION On ground, in woods and open places

Above: *These young specimens of* Amanita parcivolvata, *found growing in the center of a gravel driveway, are commonly known as the "False Caesars' Mushroom."*

Amanita parcivolvata
▶ **False Cæsar's Mushroom**

Formerly known as *Amanitopsis parcivolvata*. Cap orange or red fading on the margin with white to yellow cottony patches; the margin is striate; bell-shaped, becoming expanded when old and then the surface may be flat or sunken; 1 to 5 inches broad; flesh white.

Gills yellow; free from stem; crowded.

Stem yellow; without a ring, slightly bulbous at the base; powdery; 1 to 5 inches long; 0.25 to 0.50 inch thick.

Spores white; elliptical; .10 to 14 x 6.5 to 8 microns long.

The species is more common in southeastern North America and is as beautiful as the Cæsar's Mushroom. Mostly found on disturbed ground, lawns and woods.

COMMON NAME False Cæsar's Mushroom

SEASON July–September

EDIBILITY Unknown edibility

LOCATION On ground, in woods; scattered

Above: Amanita rubescens *is found in mixed woods; often variable in form, it can have sunken wavy edged caps.*

Amanita rubescens
▶ The Blusher

Cap egg-shaped at first, then convex and later expanded; surface adorned with thin flaky or mealy warts; variable in color but always tinged with reddish or with brownish-red, changing slowly to reddish when bruised; pleasant odor and taste; margin smooth or with slight furrows; flesh white, changing slowly to reddish when bruised; 3 to 5 inches broad.

Gills free from stem or adjacent to it, running slightly down the stem; close together; white; characteristically chalky white when dry.

Stem with a ring or collar on its upper portion; bulbous at the base; with small scales; whitish, but generally with dull reddish stains especially near the base; stuffed; 3 to 6 inches long. Spores white; ellipsoid; smooth; glassy (hyaline); 10 to 11 by 6 to 7 microns in diameter.

COMMON NAME The Blusher

SEASON July–October

EDIBILITY Edible, but eat not

LOCATION Found commonly on the ground in woods and groves from Maine to Alabama and west to Ohio. Also found in California

This white-spored genus has gills attached to the stem by their inner edge. The stem usually has a collar, but there is no wrapper or cup at the base as in the genera *Amanita*. The stem is fibrous and not easily separable from the substance of the cap, another feature in which this genus differs from *Amanita* and also from *Lepiota*.

Armillaria mellea
▶ **Honey Mushroom, Honey-Colored Armillaria**

"The honey-colored *Armillaria* is very plentiful and extremely variable. The stem may be of uniform thickness or thickened at the base or even narrowed almost to a point here. In one variety it has a distinctly bulbous base, in another a tapering base like a tap root, which penetrates the earth deeply. The plants rarely appear plentifully before the last of September." Charles H. Peck.

"Abundant on stumps and buried roots of both deciduous trees and evergreens, on which it grows as a parasite, appearing in dense clusters in autumn. . .the shining brown cords or rhizomorphs seen in dead logs and stumps." Dr. W. A. Murrill.

"Its clustered habit, the usually prominent ring on the stem, and the sharp, blackish, erect scales which usually adorn the center of the cap, mark it as an easy plant to determine in most cases. The colors and markings however, vary greatly, so that some of the forms are very puzzling." G. F. Atkinson.

Cap convex to expanded; pale honey yellow to dark reddish-brown; very variable in color and form but once known is easily recognized. With minute tufts of brown or blackish hairs, but sometimes smooth; when old sometimes with minute radial furrows (striate) at the margin; center sometimes prominent (umbonate); flesh white or whitish, somewhat acrid and unpleasant to the taste (raw); 1 to 6 inches broad.

Gills attached to the stem or even extending down it; white or whitish, becoming discolored or spotted with age.

Stem adorned with a collar or ring in its upper portion; this ring is variable, sometimes white and cottony or thin and webby and disappearing when old; (stem) honey-colored, reddish-brown, or dirty brown below, paler above; firm; fibrous; spongy within; usually having flakes or scales upon it below the ring; 1 to 6 inches long;, 0.25 to 0.75 inches thick.

Spores white; elliptic; smooth; glassy (hyaline); 7–10 m. long.

Above right: *A cluster of* Armillaria mellea *growing from dead wood is the variety with a reddish-honey color. This color variety of* Armillaria mellea *is yellowish -honey colored with a long stem.* **Below right:** *This group of* Amanita virosa, *a deadly poisonous mushroom, was found growing on a lawn, it typically is found on the ground in the woods.*

COMMON NAME Honey Mushroom, Honey-Colored Armillaria

SEASON Summer–Autumn

EDIBILITY Edible

LOCATION On ground or on decaying wood: in woods or in cleared land; solitary or in groups, tufts or clusters

Cantharellus
Genus

The genus *Cantharellus* is distinguished by the character of the gills (which are not true gills) but are an obtuse or blunt edge and are mostly forked or branched. They can be generally narrow, thick or almost smooth. In appearance the species are not unlike species of *Clitocybe*, as the gills extend down the stem (decurrent), but their thick branching habit and blunt edge give the plant a distinct character. In many species the gills look like veins, folds or wrinkles.

Cantharellus cibarius
► Chanterelle, Golden Chanterelle

The chanterelle is beautiful in color if not in shape and is most easily recognized. Its color is a uniform rich egg-yellow, which is very constant. This extends to all parts of the plant except the inner flesh, which is white.

"The orange chanterelle or false chanterelle, *Hygrophoropsis aurantiaca*, is the only species liable to be mistaken for the edible chanterelle. It may at once be recognized by the orange color of its gills, which are also thinner and more close and are regularly and repeatedly forked. The color of its cap is a paler and more dingy yellow, varied with smoky-brown tints." Charles H. Peck.

Cap fleshy; firm; convex, becoming expanded or depressed at the center (funnel-shaped); smooth; chrome (egg) yellow; the margin when young turning in but later spreading and often wavy or irregular; flesh white; taste when raw often a little pungent or acrid; 1 to 3 inches broad.

Gills or spore bearing surface, far apart; thick; narrow; forked; extending down the stem (decurrent); yellow.

Stem variable in length; firm; smooth; solid; yellow; often curved; sometimes tapers downward. By some, it is considered as good as the cap for food; 1 to 2 inches long, 0.25 to 0.50 inch thick.

Spores pale yellowish; elliptic; .0003 inch to .0004 inch long.

Right: *A group of* Cantharellus cibarius *growing under oak trees develop a characteristic funnel shape with ridges and crossveins instead of true gills.*

COMMON NAME Chanterelle, Golden Chanterelle

SEASON June–September

EDIBILITY Edible

LOCATION On ground in woods and open places; commonly in groups, but sometimes in curved lines (partial fairy rings)

Above: Cantharellus cinnabarinus *grow in mixed woods, they are cinnabar red in color and can be found in large numbers.*

Cantharellus cinnabarinus
▶ Cinnabar Chanterelle

Cap firm; convex or slightly depressed in the center; often irregular in shape, with a wavy or lobed margin; smooth; cinnabar red; flesh white; size, 0.50 to 1.50 inches in diameter.

Gills or spore-bearing surface, narrow; blunt on edges; far apart (distant); branched or forked; extending down the stem (decurrent), red like the surface of the cap.

Stem equal or tapering downward; smooth; solid or stuffed; red like the cap.

Spores white; elliptic; .0003 to .0004 inch long, .00016 to .0002 inch broad.

The Cinnabar Chanterelle is readily recognized by its color. It is externally red in all its parts, the interior only being white. The color is quite constant, but in some instances it is paler and approaches a pinkish hue. It is apt to fade or even disappear in dried specimens.

This mushroom sometimes occurs in great abundance, which adds to its importance as an edible species. The fresh plant has a tardily and slightly acrid flavor, but this disappears in cooking.

It is a small species but often quite irregular in shape. Small specimens are more likely to be regular than large ones. Sometimes the cap is more fully developed on one side than on the other. This makes the stem eccentric or in some cases almost lateral.

COMMON NAME Cinnabar Chanterelle

SEASON July–September

EDIBILITY Edible

LOCATION In woods and open places

Cantharellus
Genus

Above: *These* Cantharellus infundibuliformis *are found in large numbers growing in wet lowlands near or in sphagnum moss.*

Cantharellus infundibuliformis
▶ Funnel-form Chanterelle

"Its cap is more highly colored when moist and becomes paler with the loss of moisture. In some specimens the margin becomes wavy or folded and has a very irregular appearance. In maturity, the gills appear frosted or covered with a minute whitish dust—one of the traits that distinguish this species from the Yellowish Chanterelle." Charles H. Peck.

Cap thin; broadly convex in youth, becoming funnel-shaped when older. Margin often irregular. Looks damp dirty brown, brownish- or dingy-yellow when moist; sooty brown, brownish-yellow, grayish-brown and slightly scaly when dry; 1 to 2 inches broad.

Gills narrow; far apart; extending down the stem; irregularly forked or branched; yellowish or slightly ashy, becoming dusted when old or in drying. Stem slender; smooth; hollow; yellowish; 1 to 4 inches long.

Spores white; broadly elliptic or globular; .00035 to .00045 inch long.

COMMON NAME Funnel-Form Chanterelle

SEASON June–October

EDIBILITY Edible

LOCATION On ground; damp woods or mossy, shaded swamps; in groups, sometimes in tufts

Gomphus
Genus

Gomphus floccosus
▶ **Floccose Chanterelle**

The following description is interesting in that this mushroom used to be considered a good edible mushroom, but now has the reputation for causing gastrointestinal upset. This species; cannot be recommended for the table.

"The floccose chanterelle is a large and very distinct species. There is nothing with which it can easily be confused. When young it is narrowly club-shape or almost cylindric, but soon becomes trumpet-shaped. My trial of its edible qualities was very satisfactory, and I consider it a very good mushroom for the table." Charles H. Peck.

Cap funnel-form or trumpet-shaped;deeply excavated; firm; rather thin; surface somewhat scaly; yellowish inclining to rusty; 2 to 4 inches broad at the top, 3 to 6 inches long.

Gills or spore-bearing surface, narrow; thick; blunt on the edge; repeatedly forked and branched so that the lower surface of the cap has a coarse network of them; gills and interspaces rusty or yellowish; extending down the stem.

Stem short; smooth or hairy; sometimes elongated and bent.

Spores rust-colored; elliptic; .0005 to .0006 inch long by .0003 inch broad with a small oblique point at one end; usually with one nucleus.

Right: The Gomphus floccosus *are related to chanterelles however they can cause gastric upset and are not recommended as an edible.*

COMMON NAME Floccose Chanterelle

SEASON July–September

EDIBILITY Causes gastric upset

LOCATION On ground in woods; in groups

The white-spored genus *Clitocybe* differs from *Tricholoma* in the character of the gills. They are attached to the stem at thei inside edge as in that genus, but are not notched or excavated there, as is *Tricholoma*. The gills of *Clitocybe* generally extend down the stem (decurrent). The flesh is continuous with the stem, therefore the cap is not easily separated from it.

Some are poisonous and the majority are unknown as to their edibility; however none are known to be fatally poisonous.

Clitocybe infundibuliformis
▶ Funnel Form Clitocybe

Cap convex and slightly knobbed at center when young; funnel-shaped when mature; margin thin and minutely silky; dry; reddish or pale tan color, fading with age; flesh white; 2 to 3 inches broad.

Gills thin; moderately close together; extending down the stem (decurrent); white or whitish.

Stem generally tapering upward; generally pithy or spongy; soft; elastic; color of cap or paler; 2 to 3 inches long.

Spores white; 5 to 6 by 3 to 4 microns in diameter.

Right: *These small specimens of* Clitocybe infundibuliformis *are commonly found under conifer or oak trees, they are also known as* Clitocybe gibba.

COMMON NAME Funnel Form Clitocybe

SEASON July and August

EDIBILITY Edible

LOCATION On ground; among fallen leaves in woods; single or scattered, rarely tufted

Collybia
Genus

In the white-spored genus *Collybia* the gills are free from the stem or notched or curved upon their edges near the stem. The stem is either entirely cartilaginous (like gristle) or has a cartilaginous rind while the central portion of the stem is fibrous or fleshy, stuffed (pithy) or hollow. The cap is fleshy and when the plants are young the margin of the cap is incurved or inrolled, i.e., it does not lie straight against the stem as in the genus *Mycena*.

Many of the species of *Collybia* are quite firm and will revive somewhat when moistened after drying, but they are not coriaceous (leathery) as in *Marasmius*, nor do they revive so thoroughly. It is difficult, however, to draw the line between the two genera.

Collybia dryophila
▶ **Collybidium Dryophilum, Oak-Loving Mushroom**

"An edible species of good quality. The early spring form is smaller than the more common summer and autumn form." Dr. W. A. Murrill.

"The oak-loving collybia is one of our most common mushrooms. It occurs in woods, groves, open places and pastures and appears at any time from early spring to late autumn when there is a sufficient degree of warmth and moisture. A favorite place of growth is among fallen pine leaves or under pine trees. It also grows on decaying wood. When it occurs in dense tufts the caps are usually very irregular on account of mutual pressure. The flesh is slightly tough but is agreeable to the taste and perfectly harmless." Charles H. Peck.

Cap pale or dark tan, yellowish or chestnut; rather tough; convex to nearly plane, sometimes depressed at the center; edge often wavy, turned in when young; surface smooth and dry; flesh thin, white, 0.50 to 2 inches broad.

Gills adnexed (adjacent to but not attached to stem) or with a bend or tooth near the stem; whitish or rarely yellowish; rather near together.

Stem cartilaginous (like gristle); smooth; brown; hollow, or stuffed (pithy) in lower portion; sometimes bulbous at base; 1 to 3 inches long.

Spores white; elliptic or egg-shaped; smooth glassy (hyaline); 5 to 7 by 4 to 5 microns in diameter.

Right: *A group of common Collybia dryophila growing under conifer trees, they are also found near oak.*

COMMON NAME Collybidium Dryophilum, Oak-Loving Mushroom

SEASON May–October

EDIBILITY Edible, taste nutty

LOCATION On ground or rarely on decayed wood; in woods and pastures; in groups or slightly tufted

Family

Above: *This group of* Collybia oregonensis, *found in the redwood forests of the Pacific coast, has a rooting stem and a fragrant odor of almonds.*

Collybia oregonensis
▶ Fragrant Collybia

Can be found in small groups or single mushrooms. The sweet odor is similar to almond extract. Not common with an unknown ediblity.

Cap convex to flat; smooth; somewhat viscid when moist; deep reddish-brown lighter toward the margin; thin flesh; 1 to 4 inches broad.

Gills adnexed or notched; crowded; cream to buff, sometimes stained reddish.

Stem 2 to 8 inches long, with a deep root; swollen at ground level; dry; white with reddish stains on lower section.

Spores elliptical; smooth; white to buff colored; 6 to 8 x 3.5 to 5 microns.

The look-alike redwood rooter, *Caulorhiza umbonata*, has a true tap root and a pointed umbo. The *Collybia subsulcatipes* also has a tap root and a lighter fragrance.

COMMON NAME Fragrant Collybia

SEASON October–March

EDIBILITY Edible, nutty taste

LOCATION Growing on rich humus near stumps; pacific coast of North America

Above: *This large cluster of* Coprinus variegatus, *found growing on decaying American Elm wood should not be eaten within 24 hours of the consumption of alcohol.*

Coprinus variegatus
Scaly Inky Cap

The *Scaly Inky Coprinus* inactivates an enzyme that detoxifies alcohol, causing temporary illness if eaten at the same time as anything having alcoholic content. Therefore, these mushrooms should never be eaten within 24-hours of the consumption of alcohol.

Cap egg-shaped when young, becoming expanded; grayish-brown with whitish to ochre loose scales; flesh tan, 1 to 3 inches broad.

Gills free; close together (crowded); white when young, soon becoming purplish-brown then black and liquefying.

Stem fibrous; hollow in age; white or whitish; 2 to 5 inches long 0.25 to 0.375 inch wide.

Spores elliptical; black; 7.50 to 10 x 4 to 5 microns.

COMMON NAME Scaly Inky Cap

SEASON Late summer and autumn

EDIBILITY Edible with caution

LOCATION In clusters on hardwood especially ash and elm in woods

Above: Coprinus atramentarius *grow in clusters on the ground and are common in gardens. They contain a substance that prevents alcohol from being processed and cannot be eaten within 24 hours of the consumption of alcohol.*

The genus *Coprinus* is easily distinguished from all others by the character of the gills of the mature plant. They assume a black color and slowly dissolve into an inky fluid which, in the larger plants at least, falls to the ground in drops. The thin caps of some species also partly or wholly waste away in this manner. This black fluid, sometimes used as a poor substitute for ink, has given these plants the name of "inky fungi."

A ring is present on the stem in some species. Some of the plants literally grow up in a night and perish in a day. Many inhabit dung or manure heaps, as the name of the genus implies. Most of them are so small, thin and perishable that they are not valuable as food. Even the larger ones have thin caps, and those

deemed edible should be gathered young and cooked promptly if used as food. The species described below are common and edible.

Coprinus atramentarius
▶ **Inky Coprinus**

Also called Common Inkcap or Alcohol Inky. This *coprinus* species inactivates an enzyme that detoxifies alcohol, and therefore should never be eaten within a 24-hour period of the

COMMON NAME Inky Coprinus, Common Inkcap, Alcohol Inky

SEASON Late summer–autumn

EDIBILITY Edible with caution

LOCATION In clusters in rich soil, in gardens, waste places or in woods

Family

consumption of alcohol to avoid a temporary illness.

"The cap is sometimes suffused as if with a bloom (powder). If intended for the table it must be cooked as soon as brought to the house." Charles H. Peck.

"This excellent edible species is quite common in rich soil on lawns and elsewhere during late summer and autumn. As it appears in close clusters, it may be obtained in greater abundance than the shaggy-mane (Coprinus comatus)." Dr. W. A. Murrill.

"Sometimes the cap is entirely smooth. Other forms present numerous small scales on the top or center of the cap. In others the delicate tufts (scales) cover more or less the entire surface, giving the plant a coarsely granular aspect. This is perhaps the more common appearance, at least so far as my own observation goes. But not infrequently one finds forms which have the entire outer surface of the cap torn into quite a large number of coarse scales, and these are often more prominent over the upper portion. Fine lines also mark the entire surface of all the forms, especially toward the margin, where the scales are not so prominent. The marginal half of the cap is also frequently furrowed." G. F. Atkinson.

Cap egg-shaped when young, becoming expanded; smooth or with a few faint spot-like scales in the center; grayish-brown, often with a yellowish tint, blackening when old; margin sometimes irregularly notched or lobed; flesh white, soon liquefying; 1 to 3 inches broad.

Gills close together (crowded); white when young, soon becoming black and liquefying.

Stem rather slender; smooth; hollow; white or whitish; sometimes with a slight vestige of a ring near the base, but it soon disappears; 2 to 4 inches long.

Spores elliptical; black; .0003 to .0004 inches long.

The inky coprinus is much less attractive than the shaggy *coprinus* (*Coprinus comatus*).

The form growing in woods is generally smaller and more beautiful than that growing in open places.

Coprinus comatus
▶ **Shaggy-Mane Mushroom,
Shaggy Coprinus,
Horse-Tail Mushroom**

Cap at first oblong or nearly cylindrical, becoming bell-shaped or expanded and splitting on the margin; whitish, adorned with scattered yellowish scales; turning to a black liquid when old; 1.50 to 5 inches long before expansion; the scales make the shaggy appearance which gives it its name.

Gills white and closely crowded together at first; soon pinkish, reddish or purplish tints appear, which quickly turn to black; sometimes all these tints may be seen at one time on one plant; dissolving into a black liquid.

Stem white; smooth; hollow; rather long; smooth or with minute fibers; in the young plant it is furnished with a ring or collar which is movable or but slightly adherent. This collar is easily destroyed and has often disappeared at maturity; 3 to 5 inches long; 0.25 to 0.33 inches thick.

Spores black; elliptic; .0005 to .0007 inches long.

"The shaggy coprinus or maned agaric as it is sometimes called, is one of the largest and finest species of the genus. It is very tender and digestible and scarcely inferior to the common mushroom in flavor, though some think it is improved in flavor by cooking a mushroom or two with it. It is fit for the table only before the gills have assumed their black color, but even after that it is sometimes used in making catsup.

"When young it is very sapid and delicate, cooked quickly with butter, pepper, and salt, it is excellent; in flavor it much resembles the common mushroom, to which it is quite equal if not superior; it is clearly more digestible and less likely to disagree with persons of delicate constitutions." Charles H. Peck.

"The shaggy-mane is a very conspicuous object on lawns in autumn, although it is not so abundant as might be desired. On account of its peculiar shape and decided colors, a single specimen rarely fails to attract attention. It is considered one of the very best of the edible fungi." Dr. W. A. Murrill.

Above right: Coprinus comatus *will deliquesce into black ink leaving a long white stem.* **Below right:** *The common* Coprinus comatus *grow in groups as shown, often on lawns and edges of paths.*

COMMON NAME Shaggy-Mane Mushroom, Shaggy Coprinus, Horse-Tail Mushroom

SEASON Late summer and autumn

EDIBILITY Edible

LOCATION On ground, in pastures, waste places or dumping grounds in close groups

Coprinus micaceus
▶ Glistening Coprinus, Glistening Inkcap

"The Glistening Coprinus is a small but common and beautiful species. Several successive crops often come about a single stump in one season. These tufts are sometimes very large and composed of very many plants crowned closely together. Sometimes the caps crack into small areas, the white flesh showing itself in the chinks.

In tenderness and delicacy it does not appear to be at all inferior to the Shaggy Coprinus and it certainly is harmless." Charles H. Peck.

"In wet weather this coprinus melts into an inky fluid, but in quite dry weather it remains more or less firm and sometimes it does not deliquesce at all, but dries with all parts well preserved, though much shrunken." G. F. Atkinson.

Cap somewhat bell-shaped or expanded; thin; marked with impressed radiating lines or striations from the margin to or beyond the middle; buff-yellow or tawny yellow; center smooth and often a little more highly colored than the rest; sometimes glistening with minute particles when young but these are not often noticeable and when present in young specimens they disappear when the plant is mature; the margin is often notched or lobed and wavy and splitting when the cap expands; when old the color is brownish or dirty, especially if wet; 1 to 2 inches broad.

Gills crowded together; whitish when young, soon becoming pinkish tinted and later, brown and black and liquefying.

Stem white; slender; fragile; smooth; hollow; 1 to 3 inches long.

Spores brown, which is unusual in this genus (others have black spores); elliptical; .00025 to .0003 inch long.

Right: A cluster of Coprinus micaceus *growing in a lawn on the remnants of a stump which causes it to appear to be a terrestrial mushroom.*

COMMON NAME Glistening Coprinus, Glistening Inkcap

SEASON May–November

EDIBILITY Edible

LOCATION On ground or on decaying wood; in clusters

Cortinarius
Genus

This genus is distinguished by the yellowish-brown, rusty, clay color of the spores and by the webby character of the veil which, in the young plants, stretches between the stem and the margin of the cap. In many species these fine webby filaments are so numerous that they at first conceal the gills, but they mostly disappear with advancing age, and leave little or no trace of a collar upon the stem.

In the young plants of this family the color of the gills is generally quite unlike that of mature ones, The mature gills become dusted by the spores which collect upon them and assume their color so that the mature plants of all of the species of this genus are colored similarly. It is therefore of the utmost importance in identifying specimens of *Cortinarius* to know the color of the gills of both the young and old plants.

The gills of all species of *Cortinarius* are attached to the stem at their inner end and usually their free edges are sharply bent or toothed near the stem (emarginate).

The plants of this genus are usually found growing within or at the borders of woods.

This is one of the largest groups of mushrooms, with more than 500 species in the genus; some are edible but others are deadly poisonous. Since accurate identification can be difficult and the toxins can accumulate in the human body, it is not recommended to gather them for the table.

Cortinarius armillatus
▶ Bracelet Cort

This *Cortinarius* is one of the edible species of the genus, however it is not recommended since there are deadly cortinarius species and because of the difficulty in identifying them accurately. This is one of the very common corts that typically are found in great numbers throughout wooded areas.

Cap large; bell-shaped to flat in maturity; margin sometimes curved with remnants of the partial veil; reddish-tan to reddish-orange; smooth or with fine fibers; moist to sometimes dry.

Gills distant; attached; broad; pale cinnamon to deep rust colored.

Stem club-shaped and nearly bulbous; solid; 3 to 6 inches long and 0.50 to 1.50 inches wide; decorated with 1 to 4 red bands around the middle of the stalk; partial veil is whitish and cobwebby.

Spores elliptic with warts 8 to 12 microns long by 5 to 7 microns wide; brown with a rusty spore print.

Right: *A specimen of* Cortinarius armillatus *shows the distinctive red banding of the stem.*

COMMON NAME Bracelet Cort

SEASON August–October

EDIBILITY Edible, but eat not

LOCATION On ground in wooded areas, especially near birch or pine trees, singly or in groups

Family

Cortinarius corrugatus
▶ **Corrugated Cortinarius**

"The *Corrugated Cortinarius* is a well-marked and easily recognized species. Though the color of the pileus (cap) is variable, its viscid, corrugated surface and the viscid bulb of the stem afford easily recognized characters. Sometimes the wrinkles join with each other in such a way as to give a net-like appearance. The margin in young plants is incurved. The bulb in the young plant is even broader than the cap, which then appears to rest upon it. The plants sometimes grow in considerable numbers" Charles H. Peck.

Cap with coarse corrugations or furrows; broadly bell-shaped or very convex; sticky (viscid) when moist; bright yellow, reddish-yellow, tawny or rusty; flesh white; 2 to 4 inches broad.

Gills close together; pallid when young, turning tawny or rusty-colored when mature; uneven on their free edges; attached to stem (adnate).

Stem long; cylindric; hollow; bulbous at the base; paler than the cap except the bulb which is the color of the cap and sticky (viscid) 3 to 5 inches long.

Spores rusty (ochraceous); broadly elliptic; rough; .00045 to .00055 by .0003 to .0004 inch in diameter.

Right: *These* Cortinarius corrugatus, *found growing on soil in mixed woods among leaf debris, have the characteristic wrinkled caps.*

COMMON NAME Corrugated Cortinarius

SEASON June–September

EDIBILITY Edible

LOCATION On ground in woods and bushy places; in groups (gregarious)

Entoloma
Genus

The stems of mushrooms belonging to this genus have neither ring nor cup. The gills are attached to the stem and sometimes extend down it and become pink when old by being dusted with the rosy-colored spores. In this respect the plants might be confused with specimens of the genus *Agaricus*. As many *Entolomas* are poisonous, errors might have serious consequences. The difference is that in the edible mushrooms of the genus, *Agaricus*, the gills are pink when the plant is young and grow brown and then black as the plant ages, while in the *Entolomas*, the gills remain pink to the last.

Mushrooms of the genus *Pluteus* have also pinkish gills but they are free from the stem and never attached to it as are those of *Entoloma*.

Entoloma abortivum
▶ **Abortive Entoloma**

The Abortive Entoloma takes this name because it is usually found growing with an imperfectly developed subglobose (slightly globular) form in which there is no distinction of cap, stem or gills. It is simply an irregularly rounded mass of cellular tissue of a whitish color, originally described as a subglobose umbilicate (having a pit or depression at its center) downy mass. It is not always umbilicate nor is the surface always downy. It grows singly or in clusters of two or more.

The well developed form is generally a clean neat-appearing mushroom but one of a very modest unattractive grayish colored cap and stem, with gills similarly colored when young, becoming salmon-hued when mature. The farinaceous taste and odor are not always distinct unless the flesh is broken. . . . (picked) in good condition and properly cooked it is an excellent mushroom. The abortive form is thought by some to be even better than the ordinary form." Charles H. Peck.

Cap fleshy; firm; convex, plane or slightly depressed at the center; usually regular on the margin but sometimes wavy and irregular; dry; silky when young, smooth when old; gray or grayish-brown; flesh white; taste and odor slightly branny; 2 to 4 inches broad.

Gills thin, close together; attached to the stem (adnate) or extending some distance down the stem (strongly decurrent); whitish or pale gray when young, changing to salmon color with advancing age.

Stem solid, slightly downy or fibrous; color of the cap or paler; 1.5 to 3 inches long, 0.25 to 0.5 inch thick.

Spores salmon-pink; angular; with one nucleus; 8.5 to 10 by 6 to 7.5 microns in diameter.

Right: *This example of tightly clustered* Entoloma abortivum *show the results of being attacked by the* mycelium *of* Armillaria mellea.

COMMON NAME Abortive Entoloma

SEASON August–October

EDIBILITY Edible

LOCATION On rich earth or much-decayed wood; in woods or in open places; commonly in groups, sometimes single, sometimes tufted

Flammulina velutipes
▶ **Velvet Foot, Winter Mushroom**

The Velvet Foot is one of the few mushrooms that appear late in the season. It has even been called a winter mushroom because it is possible to find it in mild thawing weather in winter. It sometimes develops in spring also. It is easily recognized by its viscid (sticky) tawny cap, its velvety stem and tufted mode of growth. In very young plants the stem is whitish.

"Its edible qualities are not inferior to those of the rooted collybia. Its flesh is more tender and quite as agreeable in flavor. It is well to peel the caps before cooking in order to free them from adhering particles of dirt." Charles H. Peck.

"This species is remarkable for its late appearance, being often collected in the winte. It grows on stumps and dead trunks near the gound, and is easily recognized by its viscid, yellowish cap and velvety stem." Dr. W. A. Murrill.

Cap rather thin; convex or plane; smooth; sticky (viscid); reddish yellow or tawny, sometimes yellowish on the margin and darker at the center; sometimes crowded into irregular shapes 1 inch or more broad, larger when not growing in tufts.

Gills broad; rather far apart ; rounded near the stem; adjacent but not attached to the stem (adnexed); white or tinged with yellow.

Stem firm; pithy (stuffed) or hollow; brown or tawny brown; velvety hairy when mature; 1 to 4 inches long.

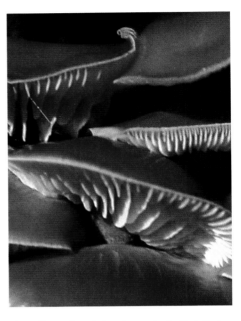

Above: Flammulina velutipes *close-up showing the brilliant cap color reflecting the gills of the mushroom above it.*
Right: *A spectacular cluster of* Flammulina velutipes, *this mushroom is found in late fall and during the winter months.*

COMMON NAME Velvet Foot, Winter Mushroom

SEASON Autumn, winter and spring

EDIBILITY Edible

LOCATION On dead tree trunks, old stumps and decaying wood; in woods or groves; in tufts or clusters or scattered

Galerina
Genus

The genus *Galerina* have small to medium sized species that usually grow among mosses and decaying wood. The spore prints are yellowish-brown to rusty brown. The gill edges are often whitish and fringed and the stems are thin. Some species are deadly poisonous and none are known to be edible. It is a complex genus with species that are difficult to identify.

Galerina autumnalis
▶ Deadly Galerina, Autumn Galerina

This small to medium sized mushroom has the same toxins found in the deadly *Amanita* species and it is highly variable in color, gill attachment and size. Formerly known as *Pholiota autumnalis* it typically grows in the fall season and can be found among other wood-loving mushrooms. It is a deceptively harmless looking "little brown mushroom" but not very attractive and should be avoided. Use caution when gathering any mushrooms growing on wood to make sure one of the autumn *galerinas* are not included by accident.

Cap convex to nearly flat with maturity; can have a knob; smooth moist or viscid; dark brown to rusty or yellowish brown fading to light yellowish brown or buff; margin is thin and striate when moist; flesh thin brown to buff; 0.75 to 2.50 inches broad.

Gills close; attached to decurrent; highly variable; yellowish brown becoming rust colored.

Stem hollow; dry; smooth; fine whitish-gray fibers covering a brownish base color darkening towards the base with white mycelium threads; veil is membranous leaving a ring on upper stem colored with rusty spores; 1 to 4 inches long by 0.125 to 0.375 inches thick.

Spores rusty brown; elliptical; roughened with a smooth depression; 8.5 to 10.5 x 5 to 6.5 microns in diameter.

Right: *The deadly* Galerina autumnalis *is a highly variable mushroom found growing on wood often in the company of other species.*

COMMON NAME Deadly Galerina, Autumn Galerina

SEASON October–November

EDIBILITY Deadly Poisonous

LOCATION On rotting wood; often among other wood-loving mushrooms; highly variable; growing in groups or singly

Family

"In the white-spored genus *Hygrophorus* the gills of the mature plant have a soft wavy texture which distinguishes them from all others. As in the genus *Pleurotus*, the gills of some of the species are rounded or notched at the end next to the stem, but the gills of other species are decurrent, that is, they extend down the stem. Those with decurrent gills bear considerable external resemblance to the species of *Clitocybe*, but the gills are generally thicker and much farther apart than in that genus. No species of *Hygrophorus* is known to be dangerous, though two or three have been classed as suspicious." Charles H. Peck.

The waxy character . . . is the chief distinguishing character of the genus. The gills are often thick and far apart. Species with decurrent gills are similar in appearance to species of *Clitocybe* but such species may generally be distinguished by the fact that their gills are far apart and their caps and stems are sticky when moist (viscid).

Hygrophorus coccineus
► **Scarlet Waxy Cap**

Cap conical to convex; knobbed; moist; smooth; bright red fading in age; flesh thin and fragile; yellowish-orange; 0.75 to 3 inches broad.

Gills attached; almost distant; waxy; yellowish to red-orange.

Stem hollow; dry; smooth; bright red to yellowish near base; variable; 1 to 3 inches long; 0.125 to 0.375 inches wide.

Spores white; elliptical; smooth; 7 to 11 x 4 to 5 microns in diameter.

This beautifully colored mushroom is also known as *Hygrocybe coccinea*.

Right: *This brightly colored* Hygrophorus coccineus *presents a beautiful contrast against the moss of its habitat.*

COMMON NAME Scarlet Waxy Cap

SEASON July–September

EDIBILITY Edible

LOCATION On ground in wooded areas or in clearings; in groups, single or scattered

Above: Hygrophorus conicus, *shown here growing in a path, stains black when handled or bruised.*

Hygrophorus conicus
▶ Conic Hygrophorus

"This species is usually readily distinguished by its conic cap with acute apex as well as by its change of color to black on drying. It is common in moist woods and grassy places from Greenland to the Bahamas and occurs in Europe." Dr. W. A. Murrill.

Cap thin; fragile; waxy; sticky (viscid) when moist; conical, usually with an acute tip or apex, rarely with a blunt tip; the margin often lobed; sometimes there are radiating cracks on the surface of the cap. The color is variable, it may be bright red, scarlet, crimson or sulphur yellow; stains black when bruised or handled. Size, 0.50 to 1.50 inches broad.

Gills waxy, rather close together; free from the stem; broad near the outer end but narrow near the stem; yellow.

Stem yellow; hollow; 2 to 4 inches long.

Spores white; elliptical; 9 to 11 x 6 to 8 microns in diameter.

COMMON NAME Conic Hygrophorus

SEASON July–September

EDIBILITY Probably poisonous

LOCATION On moist ground in woods and open places; singly or in groups

Above: *This group of* Hygrophorus flavodiscus *grows during late fall after the first frost of the season among mosses and leaf debris.*

Hygrophorus flavodiscus
▶ Yellow Centered Waxy Cap

Cap firm; convex to expanded or plane; slimy to sticky; smooth; pale yellow or reddish center becoming whitish at the margin; 1 to 3 inches in diameter.

Gills pink to whitish; thick with thin edges; far apart (distant); extending down the stem (decurrent); waxy.

Stem short; slimy; smooth; fibrous at top; white or tinged with the color of the cap; 1 to 3 inches long; 0.25 to 0.5 inch thick.

Spores white; elliptical; smooth; 6 to 8 x 3.5 to 5 microns in diameter.

This species is not seen until after a frost in the fall and is often covered with leaves or other debris.

COMMON NAME Yellow Centered Waxy Cap

SEASON October–November

EDIBILITY Edible

LOCATION On ground in pine woods; scattered, in groups or clustered

Above: *The* Hygrophorus miniatus *lives up to its name with its small stature as shown next to a clover leaf which is larger than the cap.*

Hygrophorus miniatus
▶ **Vermilion Mushroom**

"This species is very variable in color, size and mode of growth. Specimens always fade to yellow on drying." Dr. W. A. Murrill.

"The vermilion hygrophorus is a very variable but beautiful species. Unfortunately its colors are apt to fade and its beauty to be lost in drying. It is scarcely surpassed by any mushroom in tenderness and agreeableness of flavor." Charles H. Peck.

Cap deep red, vermilion or yellow; thin; fragile; smooth or with minute scales; often with a pit at the center; convex, becoming nearly plane when mature; 0.50 to 2 inches in diameter.

Gills far apart; attached to the stem (adnate); yellow, often tinged with red or, rarely, wholly red; waxy.

Stem slender; smooth; cylindric; stuffed or hollow; polished; color of the cap or a little paler; 1 to 3 inches long.

Spores white; ellipsoid; waxy (hyaline); 8 to 9 x 4 to 6 microns in diameter.

COMMON NAME Vermilion Mushroom

SEASON June–September

EDIBILITY Edible

LOCATION On ground in woods and swamps; among mosses and leaves or on bare ground; scattered, in groups or tufts

Family

Above: *These specimens of* Hygrophorus russula *lift up the leaf debris on the forest floor during the fall season.*

Hygrophorus russula
▶ Russula-like Waxy Cap

"A pretty mushroom. The reddish color similar to that of some *russulas* as is suggested by the name. It may be distinguished from *russulas* of a similar color by the downy appearance of the edge of young caps, by the different texture of the flesh and by the different shape of the spores under the microscope. . . .It is an excellent fungus, meaty, easily cooked and of fine flavor." Charles H. Peck.

Cap 2 to 5 inches broad; fleshy; firm; pale pink, rosy red or flesh color; sticky (viscid) when moist; smooth or dotted with small scales; edge covered with fine down in young plants. Flesh white; taste mild.

Gills rounded and slightly notched near the stem; extending slightly down the stem; white, often becoming red spotted when old or where wounded.

Stem solid; thick; firm; whitish or reddish; often scaly at the top; 1 to 2 inches long.

Spores white; .00025 to .0003 inch long, .00016 inch broad.

COMMON NAME Russula-like Waxy Cap

SEASON Fall

EDIBILITY Edible

LOCATION On ground in woods; solitary or in groups or in clusters

Inocybe
Genus

Mushrooms belonging to the rusty spored genus *Inocybe* are generally of small or medium size with some shade of brown as their color; most of them grow on the ground. The gills extend to the stem but are rarely attached to it. Their caps are darker in color when young than when old. The stem is not easily detachable from the cap. The spores are brownish-rust colored, with even, angular or rough contours.

Mushrooms of this genus are difficult to identify. It is often necessary, even for experts, to make use of the microscope in distinguishing the species. The resemblance of some of the *Inocybes* to others of their genus or to mushrooms of other rusty-spored genera is so close that microscopic examination of the spores cannot be safely omitted.

Many of the species of *Inocybe* are rare or local, having been found but once, and in a single locality.

"None of the species of this genus should be eaten because some of them are poisonous and the distinctions are very difficult to make." Dr. W. A. Murrill.

Inocybe lilacina
▶ Lilac Fiber Head

This common *Inocybe* is poisonous and has a disagreeable odor. It was considered to be a variety of *Inocybe geophylla* and can be found growing near that mushroom.

Cap conical to convex with a knob; dry; silky; light lilac color sometimes pinkish-brown. 0.375 to 1.375 inches broad.

Gills attached or notched; close; grayish-lilac to dull brown;

Stem grayish-lilac to pinkish-brown; silky; with thicker almost bulbous base; cobwebby veil that does not leave a ring; 1 to 2 inches long by 0.125 inch thick.

Spores brown; elliptical; smooth; 7 to 9 x 4 to 5.5 microns in diameter.

Right: *These* Inocybe lilacina *specimens grow among coniferous needles near the pacific coast. They have an unusual coloring that is not typical among* Inocybe *species.*

COMMON NAME Lilac Fiber Head

SEASON November–March

EDIBILITY Poisonous

LOCATION On ground; growing near or in mixed deciduous or coniferous woods

Laccaria
Genus

"The species of this genus have generally been included by botanists in the genus *Clitocybe*, but they are so peculiar in their general appearance that it seems best to separate them. The gills are rather thick and far apart and are broadly attached to the stem. When mature they are powdered whitish from the abundant spores. The spores are typically globular (or nearly so) and rough." Charles H. Peck.

Laccaria ochropurpurea
Purple Gilled Laccaria

Cap purplish-brown when moist, grayish or pale tan when dry; unpolished; watery in appearance when moist (hygrophanous); convex or almost hemispheric, with decurved margin; when mature, becoming plane or slightly depressed at the center; firm; fleshy; 2 to 4 inches broad.

Gills attached to or extending down the stem (adnate or decurrent); purplish (color of the cap or paler); thick; broad; far apart.

Stem long or short; variable; cylindric or sometimes thicker in the middle, sometimes thicker at each end; fibrous; solid; color of cap or paler; 1.25 to 3 inches long.

Spores white; globular; warty; 8 to 10 microns in diameter.

This species is often very irregular and very variable in size and shape. The color of the gills is generally darker than those of *Laccaria laccata*. The cap is much darker when moist than when dry. The stem is very fibrous and firm.

Above: *This group of* Laccaria ochropurpurea *are arranged to show the varying stages of the mushroom.* **Right:** *The distinctive color of the gills gives this species its name.*

COMMON NAME Purple Gilled Laccaria

SEASON July–September

EDIBILITY Edible

LOCATION On ground in open, bushy or grassy places; solitary, rarely grouped

Lactarius
Genus

In the white-spored genus *Lactarius*, the gills exude a milky or colored juice when cut. This alone serves to distinguish the genus but there are other characteristic features.

While the flesh seems to be firm and rigid, it is nevertheless very brittle. A break is quite even, not ragged or torn. In mature plants of this genus the cap is often somewhat funnel-shaped. The gills extend down the stem, and the stem is generally short and stout.

The taste of the milk is very acrid in some species, in others mild or with an acrid after-taste. "This character helps in distinguishing the species, and it is necessary to observe it by tasting, but not swallowing the milk or flesh. . . Several of the species are edible; others are affirmed by authors to be poisonous. It is prudent to avoid the use of acrid species, for, although acridity is destroyed or dispelled by cooking, they are said to be indigestible, and are acceptable only to the strongest stomachs." Charles H. Peck.

Lactarius deterrimus
▶ Orange-Milk Lactarius

Also called Delicious Lactarius. This species, formerly called *Lactarius deliciosus*, is easily distinguished from all others in the genus by its orange-colored juice. The distinctive mottled zones on the cap are less marked in old plants, and the ground-color also fades and becomes greenish. Such plants should not be used as food. There is often a slightly acrid taste to the flesh and milk when the plant is fresh and raw.

Stem smooth; short if growing from the ground, longer if growing among mosses; sometimes tapering toward the base; of the color of the cap or paler, sometimes with a few bright orange spots; 1 to 4 inches long, 0.33 to 0.66 inch thick. The stem is usually hollow in mature plants.

Cap broadly convex when the plant is young; centrally depressed or funnel-shaped when mature; smooth; moist; yellowish, with circles or mottled zones of deeper hues; flesh whitish, stained with orange in the part nearest to the gills; 2 to 5 inches broad. Gills orange-colored, but clearer than the cap; attached to the stem or extending down the stem. This species is especially found in pine woods and mossy swamps, more likely to be found in swamps when dry weather prevents its growth elsewhere.

Odor not marked; taste often slightly acrid; orange-colored milk exudes when the plant is broken. Bruised places slowly become greenish.

Spores yellowish; globular; .0003 to .0004 inch in diameter.

Right: *This specimen of* Lactarius deterrimus *is shown in its habitat of moist mossy ground. It was known as* Lactarius deliciosus *and exudes orange latex and bruises green when handled.*

COMMON NAME Delicious Lactarius, Orange-Milk Lactarius

SEASON July–October

EDIBILITY Edible when young

LOCATION On ground in woods, and mossy swamps

Above: *These* Lactarius fragilis, *found in the redwood forest, have a sweet fragrance that persists when dried or cooked.*

Lactarius fragilis
▶ Candy Cap

This *lactarius* is distinctive because of its sweet odor and flavor. It keeps its flavor when dried and will sweeten anything it is cooked with. The similar *Lactarius camphoratus*, which grows in northeastern North America, also has these qualities and a similar appearance.

Cap convex to flat or depressed, often with a knob (umbo); dry; dark orange to cinnamon or reddish-brown without concentric zones; flesh thin; fragile with an odor of maple syrup increasing when dried; exuding scant amounts of white or watery-white milk.

Gills attached becoming decurrent; close; pale pinkish to cinnamon darkening with age; 0.875 to 2 inches.

Stem fragile; hollow; hairs at the base; color matches the cap; 0.875 to 2 0.125 inches long by 0.125 to 0.375 inch thick.

Spores white to light yellow; round with warts and ridges; 6 to 9 microns in diameter.

COMMON NAME Candy Cap

SEASON Late fall through early spring

EDIBILITY Prized edible

LOCATION On ground in woods, scattered or in groups; predominantly found near the Pacific coast and in southeastern North America

Above: *This detail of* Lactarius indigo *mushrooms shows the purplish blue hues that give the species its name.*

Above: *A group of* Lactarius indigo *found in a grassy area near mixed woods are shown in various stages of growth.*

Lactarius indigo
▶ Indigo Milky

This *lactarius* is very easily identified since it is one of very few indigo-colored mushrooms. One of the most beautiful and photogenic mushrooms to be found.

Cap convex to sunken; margin inrolled first; sticky; usually with concentric zones; indigo blue when young; maturing to silvery blue staining greenish; white flesh staining blue and exuding a scant indigo-blue latex which fades to green.

Gills attached to decurrent; close; indigo when fresh becoming paler blue in maturity.

Stem tapered toward the base; dark blue to silvery-blue with darker indigo pits; hollow; dry.

Spores cream; 7 to 9 x 5.5 to 7.5 microns; elliptical to round; with ornamentation.

COMMON NAME Indigo Milky

SEASON July–October

EDIBILITY Edible

LOCATION On soil or in grass in woods or on lawns; often in groups

Above: *This group of* Lactarius lignyotus, *found in a damp area of mixed wood, is the variety* nigroviolascens *which stains purple after the damaged area dries.*

Lactarius lignyotus
▶ **Sooty Lactarius**

Also called Chocolate Milky. "A very noticeable species, well marked by its dark-brown color and velvety appearance, its long stem and by the fact that its gills, when wounded, slowly turn a reddish color. It is an excellent edible species." Charles H. Peck.

Cap convex, plane or slightly depressed at the center; with or without a small protuberance (umbo); dry, often with wrinkles radiating from center; velvety; even or lobed at the edge; sooty-brown; flesh white; exudes scanty white milk when bruised or cut; *v. nigroviolascens* stains purple when bruised and when dried. Taste mild or slightly acrid; 1 to 4 inches in diameter.

Gills attached or extending slightly down the stem; white or creamy yellow, becoming reddish where wounded.

Stem cylindric or tapering upward; stuffed; same color as cap; 2 to 4 inches long, 0.665 to 0.335 inch thick, sometimes thicker.

Spores globular with small spines (echinulate); white; 8 to 10 microns in diameter.

COMMON NAME Sooty Lactarius

SEASON July–September

EDIBILITY Edible

LOCATION On ground, in woods in hilly or mountainous places

Family

Chlorophyllum
Genus

Mushrooms belonging to the genus *Lepiota* resemble those of the genera *Amanita* in having their gills free from the stem and in having white spores. They differ in having no removable warts on the cap and no sheath or cup at the base of the stem although it may be bulbous. There is a ring or collar on the stem. In some species the epidermis (peel) of the cap breaks into scales which adhere to the cap and this feature suggests the name of the genus which is derived from the Latin word *lepis*, a scale.

Chlorophyllum molybdites (Lepiota Morganii)
▶ Green-Spored Mushroom

This is one of the largest and most handsome of the *lepiotas*. It is very abundant in southern and southwestern North America.

Cap soft and fleshy; nearly spherical when young, convex, or even depressed at the center when mature; white, with scattered brown scales which merge together at the center. Flesh white, turning reddish and then yellowish where it is wounded. Cap 4 to 12 inches broad.

Gills broad; close together; free from the stem; white when young, green when mature.

Above: Chlorophyllum molybdites *is known as the "Green Spored Lepiota." It is the toxic look-alike for other edible* lepiotas.

Stem slightly bulbous at the base; firm; stuffed; whitish, tinged with brown; surrounded by a large ring that is often movable; 6 to 8 inches long.

Spores green when first shed, slowly turning yellow; egg-shaped or slightly elliptical; mostly with a single nucleus; 10 to 13 x 7 to 8 microns in diameter.

COMMON NAME Green-Spored Mushroom

SEASON June–October

EDIBILITY Poisonous

LOCATION On ground in open places (rarely in woods); singly or in groups, sometimes in curved lines or "fairy rings"

Lepiota procera
▶ Parasol Mushroom, Tall Lepiota

"The parasol mushroom is a very neat, graceful and attractive species. The cap sometimes becomes fully expanded but usually it maintains a convex form like an opened umbrella or parasol.

The very tall, slender stem with its bulbous base, the peculiarly spotted cap with its prominent darker colored umbo (knob) and the broad space or basin about the insertion of the stem and between it and the gills, easily distinguish this mushroom.

The parasol mushroom has been highly commended and is evidently a first-class edible species." Charles H. Peck.

"This handsome edible species is found in thin soil in meadows, pastures and open woods from New England to Alabama and west to Nebraska. It is widely distributed in Europe and Asia where it is highly esteemed as an article of food, in some places being dried in quantity for winter use. On account of its scaly cap and bulbous stem, it must be carefully distinguished from species of Amanita." Dr. W. A. Murrill.

Cap thin, with a knob or eminence at the center; adorned with brown, spot-like scales; when young, the cap is brownish or reddish-brown and somewhat resembles an egg in shape. Its peel soon breaks into numerous fragments and as the cap expands, these become separated except on and near the center of the cap; flesh soft, slightly tough and white; mild odor and flavor; 3 to 5 inches broad.

Gills white or yellowish-white; close together; their inner extremity so far from the stem that there is a clear space about it.

Stem very long in proportion to its thickness; with a rather thick, firm collar or ring which, when mature, becomes loosened and movable. Bulbous at or near the base; with scales or brownish dots below the ring at times; hollow or pithy; 5 to 10 inches long.

Spores white; large; elliptic; .0005 to .0007 inch long.

Right: *A solitary specimen of* Lepiota procera, *found growing on ground near rotting wood, has a characteristic parasol shape, soft raised scales, and a ring that will move along the stem.*

COMMON NAME Parasol Mushroom, Tall Lepiota

SEASON July–September

EDIBILITY Edible

LOCATION On ground in thin woods, in fields and pastures and by roadsides

Family

Lepiota rachodes
▶ Shaggy Parasol

This beautiful mushroom is distinctive in how it bruises and then stains, changing from bright orange to red and brown: It is also known as *Macrolepiota rachodes* or *rhacodes*. It is similar to the parasol mushroom, *Lepiota procera*, but is much more shaggy.

The resemblance to the green-spored Lepiota, *Chlorophyllum molybdites*, is enough to cause concern over a misidentification, but the spore color of this mushroom is not green. The look-alike *Lepiota josserandii* and other deadly poisonous Lepiotas are much smaller mushrooms without a large ring, however, there have been fatalities due to misidentification or perhaps carelessness. Use caution when choosing any Lepiotas for the dinner table.

Cap convex drumstick-shaped becoming almost flat with a central darker cinnamon-brown disc; when expanded, it is dry, almost furry, with fibrous, cinnamon brown scales; lighter coloring between the scales; thick white flesh staining orange when bruised or cut changing to red and finally to brown.

Gills free, close; broad; white staining brown when cut or bruised.

Stem slowly enlarging toward the bulbous base; 4 to 8 inches long; 0.40 to1 inch wide; veil white and double-edged, forming a movable ring on the stem.

Spores elliptical; smooth; 6 to 10 x 5 to 7 microns in diameter; leave a white spore print.

Above: *Detail of a single* Lepiota rachodes *showing the shagginess of this species.* **Right:** *These* Lepiota rachodes *are often found in large quantities near coniferous trees. They have felt-like scales and a movable shaggy ring on the stem.*

COMMON NAME Shaggy Parasol

SEASON September–October

EDIBILITY Edible with caution

LOCATION On ground in groups or fairy rings, single in woods chips, pine needles or leaves

"The fragments of the veil adhering to the margin of the young cap is a distinguishing feature of the genus *Naematoloma*, and is suggestive of its name. Many of the species grow on wood and are tufted (*cespitose*) in their mode of growth. The spores are brown or purplish-brown. The genus resembles in structure the white-spored genus *Tricholoma*, the pink-spored *Entoloma* and the rusty-spored *Hebeloma*. When there is a well-developed veil hanging from the margin of the cap the specimen must be carefully distinguished from *Stropharia*, on the one hand, and on the other hand, if the veil is scanty or missing, from *Psilocybe*." Charles H. Peck.

Naematoloma sublateritium
▶ **Brick-red Hypholoma; Brick-tops**

Cap dark brick-red, often paler on the margin; convex or nearly plane; smooth; dry; flesh whitish or yellowish, taste commonly bitter; sometimes mild; 1 to 3 inches in diameter.

Gills extending to the stem or attached to it; close together; whitish or yellowish white, becoming tinged with green when mature, and later, purplish-brown (from the ripened spores).

Stem cylindric or tapering toward the base; occasionally several stems grow from a common base; smooth or slightly fibrous; stuffed; some becoming hollow when old; rust-colored; 2 to 3.50 inches long.

Spores purplish-brown; 6 to 8 x 3 to 4 microns in diameter.

Specimens that are collected after frost has checked the ravages of insects, are found to be free from any bitter taste. This mushroom could also be called the winter mushroom as it can be found after a hard frost.

Left and right: *A cluster of* Naematoloma sublateritium, *found growing on buried wood in late fall and winter months during mild weather.*

COMMON NAME Brick-red Hypholoma; Brick-tops

SEASON August–December

EDIBILITY Edible

LOCATION On or about old stumps, prostrate tree trunks and on decaying wood covered with earth; commonly in tufts

Omphalotus

Genus

Omphalotus olearius
▶ Jack-o'-lantern

"The Jack-o'-lantern is an attractive fungus, forming large tufts or even patches on or about old stumps or decaying wood or buried roots. This mushroom was known as *Clitocybe illudens* and *Omphalotus illudens*.

"A beautiful but unwholesome species. It causes nausea and vomiting if eaten. It is phosphorescent. Large fresh specimens when placed in a dark place emit a glowing light." Charles H. Peck.

"From the rich saffron yellow color of all parts of the plant, and especially by its strong phosphorescence, so evident in the dark, it is an easy plant to recognize.

While the plant is not a dangerously poisonous one, it has occasioned serious cases of illness, acting as a violent emetic, and of course should be avoided." G. F. Atkinson.

Cap convex or nearly plane, sometimes depressed in the center, sometimes with a knob at the center even when this is depressed; often irregular or with the stem placed aside from the center; smooth; 3 to 6 inches broad; saffron yellow or orange yellow; flesh white or yellowish; odor strong; taste disagreeable.

Gills color of the cap; close together; extending down the stem (decurrent); narrow at each end.

Stem long, firm; smooth; solid; pithy or rarely hollow; often tapering toward the base; color of the cap or sometimes brownish toward the base; 3 to 6 inches long or even longer.

Spores white; globular; 4 to 5 microns in diameter.

Right above: *This cluster of* Omphalotus olearius *are growing from remnants of a stump in a mixed woods habitat. They can be mistaken for chanterelles and can cause severe gastric upset.*
Right below: *A young cluster of* Omphalotus olearius *growing on buried roots in a lawn.*

COMMON NAME Jack-o'-lantern

SEASON July–October

EDIBILITY Poisonous

LOCATION On or about old stumps or decaying wood or roots buried in the ground; woods and open places; in tufts or clusters

Panellus
Genus

This genus has mushrooms that have white to yellow spores and a rough texture and lateral stem if there is one present. The growth habit is on wood, and has one species noted for edibility. The spores are smooth, and sausage-to-cylindrical in shape.

Panellus serotinus
▶ Late Fall Oyster

Cap somewhat sticky or slimy when moist; varies from yellowish-green to violet-brown; incurved margin; fan-shaped; smooth to velvet texture; 1 to 4 inches broad.

Gills attached and radiating from a stub-like stem; close; light yellow to orange-yellow.

Stem lateral; short; thick; expanding from attachment to the host wood; hairy; yellow to brown; 0.25 to 0.75 of an inch long by 0.25 to 0.375 of an inch wide.

Spores sausage-shaped; smooth; clear, leaving a yellow spore print; 4.5 to 5.5 x 1.5 to 2 microns.

This mushroom was known as *Pleurotus serotinus* and is also commonly called the green oyster mushroom. It is edible, however, it can be somewhat bitter or tough without long, slow cooking.

Right: *These specimens of* Panellus serotinus, *found on wood after a first frost in the fall, are known as "Late Fall Oyster Mushrooms."*

COMMON NAME Late Fall Oyster

SEASON October–November

EDIBILITY Edible

LOCATION On dead wood; few to many in clusters; typically growing after a frost

Panus

The mushrooms belonging to this white-spored genus are leathery fungi, growing on wood. When mature they are tough and hard. Their caps shrivel when dry but revive when moist. The gills extend down the stem (decurrent) when there is one. The stem is usually attached to the cap aside from the center and in many species is found at its edge or is even lacking altogether.

Some authorities class the mushrooms of this genus in with the *Lentinus*. The principal feature that distinguishes *Panus* from that genus is the fact that the edges of its gills are entire, that is, they are not serrate or saw-toothed.

Panus strigosus
▶ Giant Panus

Cap white; covered with hairs; margin thin; 8 inches broad or larger.

Gills broad; far apart; extending down the stem (decurrent).

Stem attached to the edge of the cap; hairy like the cap.

Spores white; elongated-oblong; 11 to 13 x 3.5 to 4.5 microns in diameter.

A remarkably handsome fungus. Its creamy whiteness and short, hairy stem make it unmistakable among other tree fungi. It is edible when young but it soon becomes woody.

Right: These large caps of Panus strigosus *resemble large oyster mushroom;, however, they are too tough to be a good edible and are rarely found.*

COMMON NAME Giant Panus

SEASON September–October

EDIBILITY Harmless

LOCATION On stumps, especially oak; in clusters or singly

Pholiota is a rusty or ochraceous-spored genus. Except for the color of the spores, many of the species belonging to this genus resemble closely those fungi of other genera so that the spore color must be observed before identification can be certainly made. Its plants resemble those of *Armillaria* among the white-spored mushrooms and Stropharia in the brown-spored series. In some of the species of *Pholiota* growing upon the ground, the spores are brown, enough to cause some difficulty in deciding whether a given species should be regarded as a *Pholiota* or a *Stropharia*. Other resemblances make the species of this genus a difficult one for the beginner.

The stem and cap are continuous with each other and cannot be easily separated. The stem has a ring or collar.

Pholiota squarrosa
▶ Scaly Pholiota

Cap saffron-rust color; covered with darker, turned-up scales; fleshy; convex; dry. Flesh light yellow. 3 to 5 inches broad.

Gills attached to the stem with a tooth; close together (crowded); narrow; pale olive when young, turning rusty when old.

Stem short when young, but long when mature; tapering downward; scaly below the ring that surrounds the upper part.

Spores rusty; elliptical; .0003 inch x .00016 inch broad.

"A variable and showy species, growing chiefly in dense tufts. The scales give the cap a very rough appearance, especially in the young plant." Charles H. Peck.

Right: *These* Pholiota squarrosa *specimens grow in clusters and are found growing on wood in large quantities.*

COMMON NAME Scaly Pholiota

SEASON August–December

EDIBILITY Was considered edible, now known to cause gastric upset

LOCATION On or near wood; in clusters

Pholiota squarrosoides
▶ **Sharp-scaly Pholiota**

Cap sticky or slimy with numerous down-curled pointy dry scales; ochre to yellow-orange to brown; flesh thick white; 1 to 4 inches wide.

Gills attached and notched; close; broad; white to rust-brown.

Stem dry and silky above cottony-fibrous ring remnants of the partial veil; ochre to orangish downcurled scales below ring; 2 to 6 inches long and 0.25 to 0.625 inch wide.

Spores oval to elliptical; smooth 4 to 5.5 microns x 2.5 to 3.5 microns; brown spore print.

This *pholiota* is similar to the poisonous *Pholiota squarrosa*, its lookalike except for the sticky to slimy layer on the cap. Another look-alike is *Pholiota aurivella*, which has flattened sticky scales. It is also edible with caution.

Right: *Clusters of* Pholiota squarrosoides *can be found growing on hardwood from late summer through the autumn months.*

COMMON NAME Sharp-scaly Pholiota

SEASON September–October

EDIBILITY Edible with caution

LOCATION On wood in clusters, especially beech, birch and maple; throughout North America

Phyllotopsis nidulans
▶ **Orange Mock Oyster**

Cap orange-yellow; densely hairy or fuzzy; inrolled margin; orange flesh; 1 to 3 inches wide.

Gills orange; attached to hairy base without a stem; variable spacing close to distant; sometimes crossveined.

Spores sausage-shaped; smooth; 6 to 8 microns x 3 to 4 microns; almost colorless; spore print pinkish.

A very beautiful mushroom that is common with a very wide range over much of North America. Formerly known as *Pleurotus nidulans* or *Claudopus nidulans*.

Above: *This group of* Phyllotopsis nidulans *has a dense covering of lighter hairs against the yellow-orange cap which distinguishes it from the edible oyster mushrooms.* **Left and right:** *This view of* Phyllotopsis nidulans *shows the beautiful arrangement of its gills and growth habit on decaying deciduous wood.*

COMMON NAME Orange Mock Oyster

SEASON August–November

EDIBILITY Inedible due to offensive odor and taste

LOCATION On rotting wood, especially deciduous, usually in overlapping clusters

Pleurotus
Genus

The genus *Pleurotus* differs from *Tricholoma* and *Clitocybe* in that the stems of plants are attached to the cap at some point to one side of the center. In some species the stem is scarcely developed; in others, it is attached to the very margin of the cap. Some species of *Pleurotus* have the gills rounded or notched at their inner extremity, near the stem, as in the genus *Tricholoma*, while others have them extending down the stem, as in the genus *Clitocybe*. A distinctive character that is worthy of notice in the genus *Pleurotus* is that the plants are found on wood only. Generally their flesh is tougher than it is in those mushrooms growing on the ground. Sometimes they grow from dead spots or dead branches of living trees, often out of reach, high aboveground.

Pleurotus ostreatus
▶ **Oyster Mushroom**

"The oyster mushroom, or oyster fungus, named for its flavor, is similar to the Sapid mushroom. Though the European plant is quite variable in color, in the United States the prevailing colors are white or ashy-gray, changing to yellowish in the old or dried state. The stem, when present, is often shorter than in the Sapid Pleurotus and is often more lateral. It is sometimes hairy at the base and is sometimes absent. But the caps are clustered and overlapped very much as in that species and the gills are the same in both. Both are much more liable to be infested with insects than is the Elm Pleurotus. Both grow on decaying wood and at the same season and under similar conditions." Charles H. Peck.

Cap convex or concave; smooth; often irregular or wavy in shape; moist in wet weather; variable in color white… yellowish, ashy gray, dull lilac or even brownish; flesh white; 2 to 5 inches broad.

Gills broad and rather far apart; extending down on the stem; branching and connected with each other on the stem; whitish or yellowish; sometimes ragged or torn.

Stem usually tufted, several growing from a common base; usually white and smooth; solid; firm; attached to the cap to one side of the center or at its margin; 1 to 2 inches long.

Spores are white; oblong; 7 to 10 microns in length.

The variety, that was known as, *Pleurotus sapidus*, and is now known to be the same as *Pleurotus ostreatus*, has pale lilac spores; oblong; .00035 to .00045 inch long.

Above right: Pleurotus ostreatus *often grow in large overlapping clusters almost covering their host tree. There is another species, the orange* Mycena leaiana, *growing with these Oyster Mushrooms.* **Below right:** *A detailed view of the gill structures of a cluster of* Pleurotus ostreatus.

COMMON NAME Oyster Mushroom

SEASON June–November

EDIBILITY Choice edible

LOCATION On dead trees in crowded clusters; stems more or less united at the base; caps crowd and overlap each other; in woods and open places

Pluteus
Genus

Mushrooms of the genus *Pluteus* have pink spores. They resemble the white-spored *Lepiotas* but have no ring upon the stem. Neither have the *Plutei* a sheath or cup (volva) enveloping the base of the stem. They are the only pink-spored mushrooms whose gills are free from the stem. The stem can be detached rather easily from the cap. The gills turn pink or flesh colored as the plant grows older.

Pluteus cervinus
▶ **Fawn-colored Pluteus; Fawn Mushroom**

Cap bell-shaped when young, later becoming expanded; smooth or slightly fibrous on the surface; dingy brown, adorned with blackish fibrils, but specimens sometimes occur with the cap white, yellow, ashy, grayish-brown or blackish-brown; slightly sticky (viscid) in wet weather; 2 to 2.50 inches in diameter; flesh white; almost tasteless.

Gills free from the stem; broad; white when young, turning pink or flesh-colored when mature.

Stem cylindric or enlarged at the base; upper portion white, the lower portion colored like the cap; usually smooth; nearly solid; brittle; easily separated from the cap; 2 to 6 inches long.

Spores flesh-colored; broadly elliptic; smooth; 6 to 8 x 5 to 6 microns in diameter.

"This species is very common in New York and variable, yet it is not abundant. Usually but one or two specimens are found at a time. It grows especially on or about old stumps and prostrate trunks and may be found in wet weather from May to October. The tendency of the gills to liquefy is often shown by their wetting the paper on which the cap has been placed for the purpose of catching the spores." Charles H. Peck.

Peck wrote that, in spite of its name, he had never seen it fawn-colored.

Right above: *This group of* Pluteus cervinus *is shown in its typical habitat on decaying wood in the forest.* **Right below:** *A solitary* Pluteus cervinus *growing on buried wood in a lawn.*

COMMON NAME Fawn-colored Pluteus; Fawn Mushroom

SEASON May–October

EDIBILITY Edible

LOCATION On wood and about stumps in woods; solitary or in sparse groups

Psathyrella
Genus

Plants of this genus of black-spored mush-rooms have fragile, thin caps with striations or radial lines upon them and when young, the edge lies straight against the stem. The gills are black to sooty and are of a uniform color and not spotted as in mushrooms of the genus *Panæolus*. The species are small and can seldom be gathered in quantity. Those tested have the mushroom flavor and are val-ued for the savor they impart to less gifted species when cooked with them.

Psathyrella velutina
▶ **Velvet Psathyrella**

This edible lawn mushroom can be con-fused with other poisonous species and can absorb and accumulate chemicals sprayed on lawns. This common species is also known as *Lacrymaria velutina*.

Cap oval to convex becoming flat, some-times with an umbo; dark yellow to orange-brown; margin with hanging remnants of the veil; dense layer of flattened fibers; flesh yel-low-brown; 2 to 4 inches.

Gills attached; close; light to dark brown; whitish edges mottled with moisture droplets.

Stem smooth and whitish above fibrous ring zone; tawny and fibrous with scales below the ring; 2 to 4 inches long; 0.125 to 0.5 inch thick.

Spores elliptical; with a protruding pore at one end; 9 to 12 microns x 6 to 8 microns; black-brown spore print.

Right: *These specimens of* Psathyrella velutina *are commonly found growing in lawns.*

COMMON NAME Velvet Psathyrella

SEASON June–October

EDIBILITY Edible with caution

LOCATION On ground especially in lawns, along paths and gravel areas; in clusters or growing alone

Family

Rhodotus

Rhodotus palmatus
▶ **Netted Rhodotus**

This attractive mushroom used to be known as *Pleurotus subpalmatus*. The fine netting is raised and lighter on the younger caps, becoming thicker and losing its contrasting color with age.

Cap pinkish-orange with a whitish to cap-colored network of cracks and pits; convex with an incurved margin; gelatinous flesh; 1 to 2 inches.

Gills attached; close with crossveins; whitish to pinkish in age.

Stem off-centered red to pinkish; curved; tough fibrous texture; dry; 1 to 2 inches long; 0.125 to 0.25 inch thick.

Spores round; warted; pinkish; 6 to 8 microns in diameter.

Right: *The rare* Rhodotus palmatus *has a fine network of raised ridges on its cap, pinkish gills and an off-center stem.*

COMMON NAME Netted Rhodotus

EDIBILITY Not edible

LOCATION This distinctive small mushroom grows on wood, especially maple or elm. Scattered or in groups; uncommon

Rozites caperata
▶ The Gypsy

Cap egg- or bell-shaped, becoming expanded when mature; smooth; often whitened in the center by whitish flakes or scales; generally more or less wrinkled; thin towards the edge; yellow; flesh white; 2 to 4 inches broad.

Gills attached to the stem (adnate); often uneven on the edge; whitish, turning rusty-colored when old.

Stem stout solid; sometimes bulbous at the base; smooth or slightly flaky; white or whitish; with a thick ring; 2 to 5 inches long.

Spores rusty; slightly elliptic; .0005 to .0006 inch long .00025 to .0003 inch broad.

"This is a fine, large mushroom easily recognized by its peculiar wrinkled cap and the white frosting or flaky covering of the center of the cap. Sometimes, however, specimens may occur in which neither the wrinkles nor the flakes are present. Occasionally there is the semblance of a sheath or cup (volva) enclosing the base of the stem. The ring (annulus) is usually well-developed, white and persistent." Charles H. Peck.

"It is much esteemed in Germany and is eagerly sought as food by the common people who call it familiarly 'Zigeuner,' the gypsy." Boston Mycological Club Bulletin, 1896.

Right: *A basketful of* Rozites caperata, *commonly known as the "Gypsy Mushroom," grow on the ground near swampy areas.*

COMMON NAME The Gypsy

SEASON July–October

EDIBILITY Edible

LOCATION On ground in woods, mossy swamps and open places; scattered or somewhat grouped

Family

Russula
Genus

"This white-spored genus closely resembles the milky mushroom genus (*Lactarii*) but is easily distinguished by the absence of a milky juice. The gills of some species when young are adorned with small drops of water, but no milky or colored juice issues from wounds as is the case in the milky mushrooms. The red colors which are so conspicuous in this species are rarely seen in *Lactarius*. In the flavor of the flesh there is great similarity. In both genera many species have a mild or agreeable flavor and many others have an acrid, hot or peppery taste. This disagreeable flavor is generally destroyed in cooking so that nearly all the species that have been tried have been found to be edible, …" (However, there are a few that will cause gastric upset.) "There is no veil or collar on the stem and no cup at its base. Many species resemble each other closely." Charles H. Peck.

Russula brevipes
▶ **Weaned Russula; Short-stemmed Russula**

Cap firm, fleshy; broadly convex when young; flat-topped, with a pit at the center (umbilicate), cup or funnel-shaped when old. Surface even; white, sometimes with yellowish stains when soil has been brought up from the ground upon it. The cap has a tendency to become yellowish when old or dried. The edge of the cap is often turned downward and inward. Flesh firm; white; taste slightly peppery (acrid). Cap 2 to 4 inches broad.

Gills thin; far apart; white, or faintly greenish when old; extending down the stem; some of them branched; rather narrow.

Stem short; thick; white; smooth; 1 to 2 inches long.

Spores white; nearly spherical; .0003 to .0004 inch long by .00024 to .0003 inch broad.

"This mushroom resembles closely the peppery-milk mushroom, *Lactarius piperatus*, but is devoid of milky juice and its gill-surfaces are often tinged with glaucus-green. It is more compact and lasts longer than do most other species of *Russula*." Dr. W. A. Murrill.

Right: *A solitary specimen of* Russula brevipes *is often found with soil and leaf debris on its cap.*

COMMON NAME Weaned Russula; Short-stemmed Russula

SEASON Summer and autumn

EDIBILITY Edible

LOCATION On ground in woods; singly in groups; Maine to Alabama and west to Colorado

Russula
Genus

Russula emetica
▶ Emetic Russula

Cap fleshy; firm when young, becoming fragile when old; convex when young, growing plane or depressed at the center when mature; marked with radiating striations or furrows on the margin; sticky (viscid) when moist; rosy or blood-red, sometimes white, or fading to white when old; easily peeled; flesh white except next to the peel when it is reddish; taste very acrid (hot, peppery); 2 to 4 inches broad.

Gills broad; rather far apart; rounded near the stem; free from the stem, or nearly so; white.

Stem solid or spongy within; white or tinged with red; 1.5 to 3 inches long.

Spores white; globular; .0003 to .0004 inch broad.

"This *Russula* has a very hot peppery taste and is generally considered poisonous by European mycologists but is deemed edible and harmless by some American mycophagists. Thorough cooking probably destroys its harmful properties. I have not tried it." Charles H. Peck (1906).

"This *Russula* has a very wide distribution, is a beautiful species and is very fragile. The plant is said to act as an emetic." G. F. Atkinson.

"It is common in woods throughout Europe and the eastern United States, often growing where logs have decayed. It is distinguished by its red color, viscid surface, readily separating cuticle (peel) and very acrid taste. In addition to its acrid quality it is definitely poisonous, containing small quantities of choline, pilzatropine and probably muscarine. When taken in any quantity, it promptly acts as an emetic. It is mainly because of the existence of this species, that most specimens of Russula should be tasted (not eaten) before selecting them as food." Dr. W. A. Murrill.

Right: *This* Russula emetica, *which has a very slimy cap, is usually found in swampy areas in a mixed woods habitat.*

COMMON NAME Emetic Russula

SEASON July–September

EDIBILITY Considered poisonous

LOCATION On ground in woods and swamps; singly or in groups

Family

Russula Mariæ
▶ **Mary Russula; Purple-bloom Russula**

"Mary's Russula is easily identified by the pruinose (powdery) appearance of the surface of its cap. When moistened and rubbed on white paper it leaves a reddish stain. A few of the gills are forked near the stem. Those caps that are purplish sometimes fade as they grow old, especially at the margin." Dr. W. A. Murrill.

"This *Russula* is a beautiful, easily recognizable species, though somewhat variable in its colors, varying from deep crimson to purple. The center is sometimes more highly colored than the margin and in old purple specimens the edge is apt to fade to a whitish color and to acquire radial marks or furrows. The spaces between the gills are veinyThe taste of the flesh is mild but occasionally specimens are found in which it is slightly peppery.

"Occasionally the stem tapers downward or is pointed at the base. Forms are seen in which the stem is entirely white, but it is usually colored like the cap or a little paler than the cap, with white ends." Charles H. Peck..

Cap nearly hemispheric when young, becoming broadly convex, flat, or even depressed at the center when mature; dry; surface powdery in appearance; dark crimson or purplish, sometimes darker at the center. Flesh white except close to the peel where it is pinkish; taste mild or slightly peppery. 1 to 3 inches broad.

Gills white when young, becoming yellowish when old; close together; attached to the stem.

Stem short; stout; solid or slightly spongy at the center; colored like the cap or a little paler; usually white at each end; rarely entirely white. 1 to 2 inches long.

Spores pale yellow; globular; .0003 inch broad.

Right: *A distinctive specimen of* Russula mariae, *shows the typical purplish cap and pale rose colored stem.*

COMMON NAME Mary Russula; Purple-bloom Russula

SEASON July–August

EDIBILITY Edible

LOCATION On ground; in woods and open places

Russula

Genus

Russula rosacea
▶ Rosy russula

This very beautiful russula is also known as *Russula sanguinea*. There are many red to rosy colored russulas and they are extremely difficult to identify to species; however, not as many have a rose color on the stem.

Cap convex to flat or sunken when mature; viscid surface when moist; smooth dark to bright red-rose fading to pink with age; flesh white; brittle; 1 to 4 inches wide.

Gills attached or somewhat decurrent; close; creamy-white to light yellow; brittle.

Stem often tapering toward the base; smooth white with rose flush; hollow at maturity; 2 to 4 inches long; 0.375 to 0.625 inches thick.

Spores round or oval; ornamented; 7 to 9 microns x 6 to 8 microns; pale yellow.

Right: *This beautiful* Russula rosacea *has a miniature specimen literally growing from its cap.*

COMMON NAME Rosy Russula

SEASON September–October

EDIBILITY Not edible

LOCATION On ground, often in grassy areas near or under conifers, predominantly pine

Family

Stropharia
Genus

The mushrooms belonging to the genus *Stropharia* possess purple-brown spores; the gills are attached to the stem and the veil forms a ring on the stem, but there is no sheath or cup (volva) at the base of the stem.

Stropharia hornemannii
▶ Lacerated Stropharia

This is a very photogenic, robust mushroom with distinctive features.

Cap large, bell-shaped to convex becoming flat with a wide umbo; margin with hanging veil remnants; slimy when wet; smooth purplish-brown to gray or reddish-brown; white flesh; 2 to 6 inches wide.

Gills attached; close; broad; light gray becoming purple-brown.

Stem silky white above a distinctive skirtlike ring; thicker with white cottony scales below the ring, tapering towards the base; thick white mycelium threads can be seen at the base; 2 to 5 inches long; 0.25 to 1 inch wide.

Spores elliptical; smooth with a pore at one end; 10 to 14 microns x 5.5 to 7 microns; purple-brown.

Above and right: *These* Stropharia hornemannii, *found growing in a cluster near decaying wood, have lilac colored gills and shaggy scales on thick stems.*

COMMON NAME Lacerated Stropharia

SEASON August–November

EDIBILITY Unknown edibility

LOCATION On ground, single to many in groups under or near conifers or on decayed wood

Family

Stropharia
Genus

Stropharia rugosoannulata
▶ **Wine-cap Stropharia**

This robust mushroom is common and very striking; the cap color is variable. The unusually long season makes it a very popular edible.

Cap bell-shaped to convex then flat; wine-red to brown or fading to tan; smooth but sometimes cracking in age; white flesh; 2 to 6 inches wide.

Gills attached; crowded; broad; white to lilac becoming purplish-gray with lilac tints becoming purplish-black.

Stem widening towards a bulbous base; fibrous to smooth; white staining yellowish to brown; white mycelium at the base; white partial veil leaving a persistent ring with grooves or striations on the upper surface and cottony patches beneath; grooves extend up the stem to the gills; 4 to 6 inches long; 0.5 to 1 inch thick.

Spores elliptical; smooth with pore at one end; 15 to 19 microns x 7.5 to 10 microns; purple-brown spores that collect on the upper surface of the ring.

Above right: *These mature* Stropharia rugosoannulata *specimens are growing up through garden debris.* **Below right:** *These* Stropharia rugosoannulata *grow in wood chips in late spring and can become large and numerous.*

COMMON NAME Wine-cap Stropharia

SEASON May–October

EDIBILITY Choice edible

LOCATION On wood chips and mulch; a common mushroom in the garden or the lawn; scattered to numerous groups

Family

Stropharia thrausta
▶ **Scaly Stalked Stropharia;**
Red Capped Stropharia

This photogenic mushroom has been known as *Psilocybe thrausta* and *Stropharia squamosa v. thrausta*. An uncommon-to-rare species.

Cap brick-red to orange; convex usually with an umbo; scattered white scales that are flattened and triangular-shaped, more numerous toward the margin; flesh white; 1 to 3.5 inches wide.

Gills attached; close; gray to violet-gray, then purplish-brown; whitish edges.

Stem coated with whitish scales from the base to the ring, growing over ochre-colored background; white above a flaring ring; 2.5 to 5 inches long; 0.125 to 0.375 inch thick.

Spores elliptical with a pore that is off-center; smooth; brownish purple; 12 to 14 x 6 to 7.5 microns.

Right: Stropharia thrausta *is a rare species with a beautiful orange-red cap, typically growing in wooded areas.*

COMMON NAME Scaly Stalked Stropharia; Red Capped Stropharia

SEASON September–November

EDIBILITY Not edible

LOCATION This mushroom grows on buried wood and organic debris; in groups or clusters

Volvariella
Genus

Volvariella, a rather rare genus, takes its name from the volva or sheath or cup surrounding the base of the stem, but which entirely envelops the plant when it is young. The genus is characterized by its rosy or reddish spores, the presence of the volva or cup and the absence of any ring on the stem.

Volvariella bombycina
▸ Silky Volvaria

Cap more or less globular when young, bell-shaped and later convex when mature; beautiful white, covered with a silky down. Old specimens may appear scaly. Flesh white and not very thick; 2 to 8 inches broad.

Gills free from the stem; close together; very broad at the middle; flesh-colored; edge sometimes ragged.

Stem tapering upward; smooth; solid; white; with a large thick cup (volva) at the base; separates easily from the cap; 3 to 6 inches long.

Spores rosy pink or flesh-colored; somewhat elliptical; 8 to 10 x 5 to 6 microns in diameter.

"There is no ring on the stem but there is a volva or cup at the base. In this respect the genus *Volvariella* corresponds with the genus *Amanitopsis*, but it differs from that genus in the color of its spores. The volva is very large and thick and is usually somewhat sticky. The generic name *Volvariella*, which signifies that it has a wrapper, was given to this plant because of the large baglike cup." McDougall.

Right: Volvariella bombycina *is an uncommon species found growing on wood or mulched ground. The cap has silky hairs and pink gills, the white stem grows out of a cup.*

COMMON NAME Silky Volvaria

SEASON June–October

EDIBILITY Edible

LOCATION On rotting wood, leaf mould and richly-manured ground; worldwide in distribution; not common; singly or rarely in tufts

Family

Xeromphalina
Genus

This genus has smaller brightly-colored mushrooms with decurrent yellow to orange or pinkish gills, a dark cartilaginous stem without a veil, tough texture, and can revive when moistened. It has been split off from *Omphalina* and was known as *Omphalia*.

Xeromphalina campanella
► **Fuzzy Foot, Bell-shaped Xeromphalina**

"This is one of our prettiest woodland species, found commonly and widely distributed in Europe and North America on dead coniferous wood. Its color is rather sober but it is conspicuous by reason of its clustered habit and is attractive because of its shapely form. It may be found throughout the growing season." Dr. W. A. Murrill.

"One of the most common, widely distributed species of the genus *Xeromphalina*. It is often clustered, large numbers covering a considerable surface of the decaying log." G. F. Atkinson.

"It is easily recognized by its yellowish-red cap, dark-brown stem and the little tuft of tawny-colored hairs at the base of the stem." Charles H. Peck.

Despite the comments of Peck this small mushroom could be confused with the deadly Autumn Galerina. Cap thin; rather tough; convex with a pit or depression at the center (umbilicate); often irregular in shape; with delicate radiating lines on the surface (striate); with a water-soaked appearance when moist (hygrophanous); yellowish-rusty to dull yellow color; 0.25 to 1 inch broad.

Gills narrow, extending down the stem (decurrent), arched; connected by veins on the under surface of the cap; yellow.

Stem very slender; polished; pale brown; hollow; adorned with brown hairs at the base; 0.5 to 1.5 inches long.

Spores white; nearly elliptic; smooth; glassy (hyaline); 6 to 7 x 3 to 4 microns in diameter.

Right: *These tiny groups of* Xeromphalina campanella *are found growing on mossy logs, they are very common.*

COMMON NAME Fuzzy Foot, Bell-shaped Xeromphalina

SEASON May–November

EDIBILITY Edible, with caution

LOCATION On dead or rotten logs, stumps, etc.; in woods; in clusters

Xerula
Genus

The common feature in this group of mushrooms is the long rooting tough stem that descends into the ground as much as 7 inches. These white-spored species have a medicinal possibility indicated by their antibiotic properties.

rare and has an unknown edibility. The distinguishing features are the red edges on the gills, a rusty brown cap and reddish stains when bruised.

Xerula furfuracea
▶ Rooted Collybia

Cap thin; convex or nearly plane; sticky (viscid) when moist; grayish-brown or smoky-brown; smooth; 1 to 4 inches broad.

Gills broad; rather far apart; adjacent to but not attached to the stem (adnexed); white.

Stem long and ending below in a long root-like prolongation extension which penetrates the earth deeply; slender; firm; generally tapering upward; pithy (stuffed); 2 to 8 inches long above the surface of the ground; whitish or color of the cap.

Spores white; elliptic with a slight oblique spur at one end; .0006 to .0007 inch long, .0004 to .0005 inch broad.

The Rooted Collybia is a common species and one easily recognized if notice is taken of the lower part of the stem. This is a long slender tap-root tapering downward and generally penetrating the earth to a depth about equal to the length of the stem above the surface. The stem is generally thickest at the surface of the ground. There are two other common similar species *Xerula megalospora* and *X. furfuracea* which are edible except the stems are tough and not palatable. The third look-alike is *Xerula rubrobrunnescens* which is

Right: *This specimen of* Xerula furfuracea, *found growing near a stump, has a depressed cap with a central knob, broad gills and a long brittle tapering stem with a tap root at its base.*

COMMON NAME Rooted Collybia

SEASON June–October

EDIBILITY Edible

LOCATION On ground, in woods; scattered

Family

Common Mushrooms Other than Those With Gills

Distinguished from the gilled mushrooms previously dealt with in this book, there remain other common fleshy fungi to be described. These include the tube fungi (shelf or bracket fungi and boletes), puffballs, mushrooms with spiny protuberances on their lower surface (*hydnums*), the coral fungi (*Clavarias*), the morels and cup fungi, the stinkhorns and others.

The form of their spore-bearing surface gives to the many orders of fleshy fungi their particular appearances. Nature has provided each of the many kinds of mushroom with some special means of increasing the area from which spores may be emitted.

In the case of the mushrooms with gills, these bladelike structures furnish a fruiting surface enormously greater in area than the plant would possess without them.

The same needed increase of surface is furnished in the *Polypores* or tube fungi by a multitude of vertical cylinders, on whose inner surfaces the spores are formed, and out of lower open ends (pores) of which they are dropped for dispersal.

The spiny, hedgehog or tooth fungi cast their spores from the surfaces of the myriad little awl-like, vertically hanging teeth. In the case of the coral fungi, an augmented spore bearing surface is provided by the many erect stems that constitute each plant.

For all the spores that fall on fruitful soil, millions come to naught, but the propagation of the species continues, so careful is Nature of the species, although so careless of the individual..

Polypores and Boletes

Polypores and Boletes are those mushrooms whose caps bear little hollow tubes on the lower surface of the cap in place of gills. Boletes grow on the ground, are fleshy, soon decay and their tubes may be easily separated en masse from the cap. As a rule they have a central stem. Polypores, on the other hand, are usually shelf or bracket fungi attached to wood by the edge of the cap or by a marginal stem and their spore tubes are inseparable from the cap.

As is the case with the gilled mushrooms, spores of the tube fungi (*polypori*) are produced on an exposed surface but within the vertically placed tubes. When mature, they fall and emerge from the open ends of the tubes. While the fleshy, short-lived fungi produce their propagating spores during a few hours or days only, some of the corky or leathery polypores continue to produce spores intermittently for months, and in some cases, over many seasons.

Above: *This large specimen of* Bondarzewia berkeleyi, *found growing at the base of a tree, has shed its white spores on the surrounding vegetation.*

Bondarzewia berkeleyi
▶ Berkeley's Polypore

This fungus appears to be a group of projecting fingers emerging from the ground, then thickening before flattening out to a few large overlapping caps that are depressed in the center. The flesh is tough and thicker at first becoming 0.125 to 0.25 inch thick.

The surface is cream to yellowish-tan with concentric zones; dry; hairy or smooth, sometimes pitted and rough. 3 to 10 inches across.

The undersurface is white with angular pores that descend the thick stalk.

The spores are white and can be seen on the surrounding vegetation; round with ridges and warts; 6 to 9 microns in diameter.

The mature specimens can exceed 40 inches in width and weigh more than 50 lbs.

COMMON NAME Berkeley's Polypore

SEASON July–October

EDIBILITY Edible when young

LOCATION Near buried roots or at the base of deciduous trees, especially oak

Above: Daedalea quercina *is a thick polypore that grows on oak with deep maze-like pores.*

Daedalea quercina
▶ Oak-loving Bracket Fungus, Thick Oak Maze Fungus

A woody, coarse, shelf-fungus. Its white to grayish-brown undersurface shows large and small irregular pores, sometimes suggestive of modified gills.

The whitish, corky caps are broadly attached to the stump, thickest at the attachment, and often zoned on the upper surface. The caps are from 2 to 4 inches deep, 3 to 6 inches from side to side and 1 to 2 inches thick. Specimens become blackish when old.

Spores are cylindric, smooth, 5 to 6 x 2 to 3.5 microns in diameter, leaving a white spore print.

COMMON NAME Oak-loving Bracket Fungus, Thick Oak Maze Fungus

SEASON Throughout the year

EDIBILITY Too tough to be edible

LOCATION On oak stumps and dead trees

Above: *The polypore* Daedaleopsis confragosa, *has a maze pattern of pores that resemble gills on its undersurface.*

Daedaleopsis confragosa
▶ **Thin Maze Polypore**

A tough, textured fungus. The brown to gray, zoned caps are attached to the wood at the edge or in the middle. The caps are from 1 to 6 inches wide, 0.5 to 1 inch thick.

Its white to light-brown under surface has a gill-like maze network of elongated pores. Staining reddish pink when bruised.

Spores are cylindrical, smooth, 7 to 11 x 2 to 3.5 microns in diameter, leaving a white spore print.

COMMON NAME Thin Maze Polypore

SEASON Throughout the year

EDIBILITY Not edible

LOCATION growing on various deciduous trees, usually not oak; scattered or groups

Fistulina
Genus

This genus of tube fungi possesses some of the characteristics of Boletus and some of Polyporus. The only common species is *Fistulina hepatica*.

Fistulina hepatica
▶ Beefsteak Mushroom, Chestnut Tongue

This dark-red, fleshy mushroom has been especially abundant since the occurrence of the blight that killed the chestnut trees in the early years of the twentieth century, thus increasing the number of hosts upon which this fungus might thrive.

The botanical name *Fistulina* (little pipe or whistle) refers to the spore-bearing tubes on the lower surface of the cap. The term *hepatica* derives from the liver-like appearance of the flesh.

The cap is thick, fleshy and dark red above and the undersurface is yellowish or whitish. The typical cap is somewhat semicircular in shape with the lateral, thick, reddish stem attached to the arc at an angle. The reddish flesh is juicy and its cut section resembles that of smoked, cooked beef tongue. The upper surface when young and in moist weather is jelly-like but covered with a sticky pellicle or skin. This jelly disappears when the mushroom dries or becomes old.

The tubes are short, free from one another and cannot be pulled away from the flesh. The upper skin is easily peeled off. The cap when mature is from 3 to 7 inches broad and from 0.50 to 1 inch thick. The stem may grow to a length as great as the breadth of the cap but is usually much shorter.

This mushroom requires a longer time to mature than do many of the other fleshy fungi. Under certain weather conditions they take ten days to reach their full development. The elliptical, yellowish spores are from 5 to 6 microns in length.

The slightly acid taste of this mushroom is not pleasant to all persons but is in high favor with many. When sliced thin and fried or well broiled the acidity is not very noticeable.

The look-alike *Pseudofistulina radicata* is not edible and is smaller with a pale yellow-brown cap and a brown velvety rooting stem.

Right: *The brilliantly-colored* Fistulina hepatica *is found growing on old chestnut stumps and has a wet layer on the cap with light pinkish-colored tubes on the undersurface.*

COMMON NAME Beefsteak Mushroom, Chestnut Tongue

SEASON July–October

EDIBILITY Slightly acid taste

LOCATION Grows like a shelf upon chestnut stumps in woods

Ganoderma applanatum
▶ **Plane Brown Ganoderma;
Artist's Fungus; Shelf Fungus**

A very common perennial woody shelf fungus attached broadly by its margin to the trunk of a dead or living deciduous tree. It is usually from 2 to 8 inches broad but may attain a breadth of two feet. Its thickness may be one quarter or less of its breadth. The upper surface is crusted, smooth or irregular and marked by concentric zones, each representing a year's growth. Color, brown to grayish, sometimes covered with rusty brown spores. The extremely small pores of the smooth lower surface are whitish, and when scratched or marked become brownish. This property makes the fungus a favorite medium for drawing pictures on its lower surface.

The tube layers grow under each other, therefore increasing the thickness each year. They increase 0.25 to 1 inch thick each season, depending on the rainfall. This growth cycle can extend for decades.

Spores are elliptical with a thick double wall, 6.5 to 9.5 x 5 to 7 microns, brown to rust.

There are many similar shelf fungi that have different colored pores and more of a banded cap surface. Not all are suitable to use for drawing, since some may shrink and rot as they age or dry out.

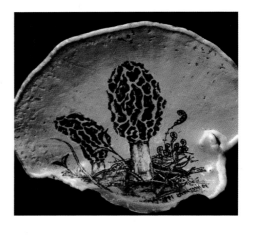

Above: *An example of the art of pyrography on the spore-bearing surface of* Ganoderma applanatum, *by Marie F. Heerkens.*
Right: *This group of* Ganoderma applanatum *has a bright white pore surface that is prized by artists for drawings. The tops of these shelf fungi are covered with chestnut-colored spores.*

COMMON NAME Plane Brown Ganoderma; Artist's Fungus; Shelf Fungus

SEASON Perennial

EDIBILITY Not edible

LOCATION Grows on wood

Ganoderma tsugae
▶ **Hemlock Varnish Conk**

The upper surface of this fungus has the appearance of having been varnished over ripples and bands.

The surface is reddish-brown with white to yellow edges when young, growing laterally from a similar-colored short stem.

Cap kidney-shaped, 2 to 12 inches wide with a stem 1 to 6 inches long and 0.5 to 1.75 inches wide. Flesh up to 1 inch thick, white, soft and corky.

Undersurface white to brownish in age with very small pores. Brown spores elliptic, with a double wall, 9 to 11 x 6 to 8 microns in diameter.

The medicinal *Ganoderma lucidum* is a lookalike that grows on deciduous wood.

Above: *Mature* Ganoderma tsugae *look as though they have a coating of varnish.* **Right:** Ganoderma tsugae *grow on hemlock, the young specimens have a lighter outer edge.*

COMMON NAME Hemlock Varnish Conk

SEASON May–November

EDIBILITY Not edible

LOCATION Grows exclusively on conifers, especially hemlocks

Grifola
Genus

A these large Grifola frondosa *specimens can be found at the base of oak trees during the fall months.*

Grifola frondosa
▶ Hen of the Woods

This fungus is a large cluster of overlapping caps that arise from a stem growing from a thick, central base.

The caps are light grayish to brown .75 to 4 inches broad, fan- or spoon-shaped with 0.25 inch-thick fibrous white flesh.

Undersurface white to cream with small pores.

The spores oval to elliptical, smooth, 5 to 7 x 3.5 to 5 microns.

The hen of the woods grows at the base of large oak trees and can weigh up to 100 lbs. This fungus was known as *Polyporus frondosus* and looks like a pile of leaves. Other edible look-alikes are the black staining *Meripilus sumstinei* and *Polyporus umbellatus* which has circular shaped caps.

COMMON NAME Hen of the Woods

SEASON August–November

EDIBILITY Choice edible

LOCATION Grows at the base of large oak trees

Family

Laetiporus
Genus

Above: *A closeup view of* Laetiporus sulphureus *showing the brightly colored overlapping caps found growing on decaying deciduous trees.*

Laetiporus sulphureus
▶ **Sulphur Polypore; Sulphur Shelf; Chicken Mushroom**

Clusters of large, brilliantly-colored, bracket-like caps of this shelf fungus overlap each other, often in profusion. Each fruiting body, attached at its margin to the host, is from 2 to 6 inches broad, flattened, often fan-shaped and wavy. The upper surface is woolly or smooth, lemon to orange in color, often somewhat zoned. The white to yellowish flesh is firm, .5 to 1.5 inches thick. The pored undersurface is light sulphur yellow with a silky sheen. Spores ovoid, waxy, 6 to 8 microns long by 3 to 5 microns broad, white.

The young, softer outer half of this fungus is best for the table and is recommended to be eaten in smaller quantities as it can be hard to digest. This fungus was known as *Polyporus sulphureus.*

COMMON NAME Sulphur Polypore; Sulphur Shelf; Chicken Mushroom

SEASON August–October

EDIBILITY Edible

LOCATION Appears on trunks of dead deciduous trees

Above: *This young specimen of* Phaeolus schweinitzii *has lighter-colored edges. Commonly known as the Dyers' Polypore, it grows on buried stumps or roots.*

Phaeolus schweinitzii
▶ Dyer's Polypore

This species is commonly used to make natural dyes for wool. The resulting colors range from a rich yellow-ochre to orange or reddish-brown to brownish-black.

Large overlapping flat caps attached to a central stalk are fuzzy, oval-shaped and tough. The color when young is rust at the center with lighter orange or yellow zones toward the margin. Sometimes wavy or lobed, 2 to 10 inches wide. The flesh is yellow to reddish-brown, 0.5 to 1 inch thick.

Undersurface yellow or greenish-yellow to orange, staining brown when bruised. The pores are very small. The central stalk is thick, 0.75 to 3 inches tall.

Spores are white, elliptic and smooth, 5 to 9 x 3 to 5 microns.

COMMON NAME Dyer's Polypore

SEASON June–November

EDIBILITY Not edible

LOCATION Grows on roots or on the ground near or on stumps or logs

Family

Above: *This polypore* Piptoporus betulinus *can become large and grows on decaying birch trees. It is light gray with tiny white pores on its undersurface.*

Piptoporus betulinus
▸ Birch Polypore

Birch Polypore was known as *Polyporus betulinus*. It has been used throughout history as tinder, to carry coals, as a razor strop, and as an anesthetic.

The smooth white or gray, corky, kidney-shaped shelf fungus can grow from 1 to 10 inches wide with an inrolled margin.

The stem is stublike, if present at all; the pores are small with white spores, 5 to 6 x 1.5 microns in diameter.

It is tough and tasteless, though not poisonous. .

COMMON NAME Birch polypore

EDIBILITY Not poisonous, but tough and tasteless

LOCATION Found growing abundantly on dead birch trees

Above: *Mature specimens of* Polyporus squamosus, *found growing on box elder, can become very large.*

Polyporus squamosus
▶ **Pheasant's Back Polypore, Dryad's Saddle**

This fan-shaped fungus can grow very large and quickly. The surface is decorated with brownish to tan scales which are arranged in a concentric pattern expanding with the growth of the fungus. 2 to 12 inches wide. A short, thick, lateral stalk is sometimes present up to 4 inches long.

The spore-bearing surface is white to cream with large-to-medium angular pores that become decurrent.

Spores white, cylindric, smooth, 10 to 18 x 4 to 7 microns.

Look-alikes include the smaller *Polyporus fagicola*, or *Favolus alveolaris* which is much smaller and has hexagonal pores.

COMMON NAME Pheasant's Back Polypore, Dryad's Saddle

SEASON Spring months

EDIBILITY Edible when young and tender

LOCATION Deciduous wood, especially box-elder (ash-leaved maple)

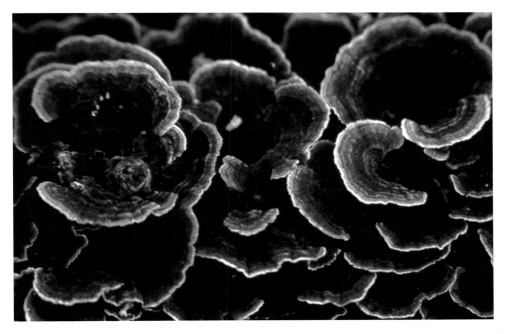

Above: Trametes versicolor *have a wide variety of colors on the upper surface and can be used to make paper.*

Trametes versicolor
▶ **Turkey Tail**

Also known as *Coriolus versicolor* or *Polyporus versicolor.* This is one of the common, thin and leathery species of *Trametes*. They grow in overlapping, wavy clusters and rosettes on dead wood to which they are attached by their margin.

COMMON NAME Turkey tail

SEASON May–December

EDIBILITY Too tough for edibility

LOCATION Grows on decaying wood

The upper surface of the cap is marked by concentric bands of various colors; grey, purple, reddish or brownish. This fungus is too tough to suggest edibility. However it can be used to make a variety of colors of handmade paper, and can be formed into jewelry.

The flesh is very thin. The white tubes are minute, giving the lower surface a smoother appearance than is usual among other polypores.

Spores are sausage-shaped, smooth and leave a white print, 5 to 6 x 1.5 to 2.2 microns.

Boletellus
Genus

Boleti

Boleti resemble, at first sight, the gilled mushrooms. Upon examining the lower surface of the cap, however, one sees a multitude of tiny holes or pores, instead of gills. The pores are the open ends of little tubes which are common to both polypores and boleti.

The chief characteristic by which one may distinguish boleti from polypores is the fact that in boleti the porous substance or mass of tubes on the undersurface of the cap may be easily removed by pressing this layer outwardly from the stem toward the margin.

"There are about 80 kinds of boletes in North America and nearly all of them are edible. A few are bitter and two are slightly poisonous; these are the sensitive bolete, which turns blue when [the broken flesh is] touched, and the lurid bolete, which has red or orange-colored tube-mouths. Many of the boletes occur in great abundance and their flavor can hardly be excelled." W. A. Murrill.

It is now known that there are almost 600 types and varieties of boletes in North America.

Any boletus, therefore, which does not turn blue when cut or broken, has not orange-colored or red tube-mouths and is mild in taste, may safely be eaten.

In preparing boletes for the table, specimens infested by larvæ should, of course, be rejected. The stems can be too tough to be edible, and the mass of tubes can be discarded. The peel, if slimy, must also be removed before cooking.

Boletellus russellii
▶ Russell's Bolete

This easily identifiable bolete is both beautiful and edible. It is uncommon to rare.

Cap convex, velvety to cracked forming patches, margin incurved, olive-gray to yellowish or reddish-brown, flesh pale yellow, 1 to 5 inches wide.

Pore surface yellow to greenish yellow, with angular pores.

Stem reddish-brown with deep grooves and shaggy ridges, curved, 4 to 8 inches long, 0.375 to 0.75 inch thick.

Spores elliptical, striate with grooves and a cleft at the top, dark olive-brown, 15 to 20 x 7 to 11 microns.

Right: Boletellus russellii *show the distinctive shaggy stems and large pores of this uncommon species. They are found in oak or pine barrens.*

COMMON NAME Russell's Bolete

SEASON July–September

EDIBILITY Edible

LOCATION Grows in groups or solitary, under oak, hemlock or oak-pine barrens

Boletus edulis

► **King Boletus; Porcini;
Cep; Steinpilz**

This is considered one of the best edible
species and is very popular. There are many
varieties of this boletus and they are all
choice edibles. The inedible lookalike
Tylopilus felleus is simply too bitter to be
eaten, but it is not poisonous, It may be easily
recognized if a small piece is tasted (not
eaten) and found to be very bitter.

The highly variable cap is light tan to reddish or brownish, from 3 to 10 inches broad
and 1 to 3 inches thick.

The flesh is firm, thick and white.

The tube layer is sunken around the stem
with very small pores, white becoming yellow
to yellowish-brown.

The solid stem is whitish when young,
becoming light brownish with a fine network
of reticulated ridges that are whitish on the
upper portion and darker below. 2 to 10
inches long, 1 to 3 inches or more thick,
occasionally misshapen with a smaller than
usual cap. The base is usually thicker to bulbous or enlarging slightly.

The spores are smooth; 13 to 19 x 4 to 6.5
microns.

Above: Boletus edulis *is a prized edible mushroom that has
pores instead of gills. It grows in mixed woods during the summer and fall.* **Right:** *A group of* Boletus edulis *showing various
stages of development.*

COMMON NAME King Boletus; Porcini;
Cep; Steinpilz

SEASON June–October

EDIBILITY A highly prized edible

LOCATION Found on ground, near
evergreen and deciduous trees

Family

Above: *The brightly-colored* Boletus frostii *often has droplets on its pores and prefers to grow in oak woodlands.*

Boletus frostii
▶ Frost's Bolete; Apple Bolete

One of the most stunning boletes, it can be locally common. It was named after Charles Frost, who helped contribute to the study of boletes in the nineteeth century. This is an amazingly deep-red-colored bolete.

Cap is sticky blood-red, convex to flat, flesh yellow, quickly staining blue.

Pore surface deep red, sometimes with yellow droplets, staining blue.

Stem red, dry, with a deeply webbed reticulate surface, staining blue, yellowish toward the base. 1.5 to 5 inches long 0.5 to 1 inch thick.

Spores elliptic, smooth, olive to brown, 11 to 15 x 4 to 5 microns.

COMMON NAME Frost's Bolete; Apple Bolete

SEASON June–October

EDIBILITY Edible, though some gastric upset has been reported

LOCATION Grows on ground in oak woods, scattered or in groups

Above: *This specimen of* Boletus parasiticus *grows from its host species,* Scleroderma citrinum, *which is known as the "Pigskin Poison Puffball."*

Boletus parasiticus
▶ **Parasitic Bolete**

An unusual bolete in that it only is found on *Scleroderma citrinum*, a poisonous puffball that it parasitizes. It is found growing solitary or in groups, and is somewhat common.

Cap convex, dry, olive to brown, flesh yellowish, 0.75 to 3 inches wide.

Pore surface yellow to olive-brown, with small angular pores, bruising ochre.

Stem yellowish to light brown, curved, 1 to 2.5 inches long, 0.25 to 0.5 inch thick.

Spores elliptical, smooth, olive-brown, 12 to 18 x 3.5 to 5 microns.

COMMON NAME Parasitic Bolete

SEASON July–September

EDIBILITY Poisonous

LOCATION Grows as a parasite on *Schleroderma citrinum*

Above: *A solitary specimen of* Leccinum aurantiacum, *found in mixed woods, grows in late summer and through the fall season.*

Leccinum aurantiacum
▶ **Red-capped Scaber Stalk; Orange-capped Bolete**

The cap is convex to flat in age, orange to brick red, dry. The flesh is white, staining pinkish to gray when bruised or cut, 2 to 8 inches wide.

The tubes are long but sunken near the stem; whitish when young, becoming grayish or brown with circular pores.

The stem has buff-colored scabers that darken to blackish-brown over a whitish background. 4 to 6 inches long and 0.75 to 1 inch thick.

Spores elliptical, smooth, yellow-brown, 13 to 18 x 3.5 to 5 microns.

COMMON NAME Red-capped Scaber Stalk; Orange-capped Bolete

SEASON August–September

EDIBILITY Edible

LOCATION On ground in woods, scattered-to-numerous

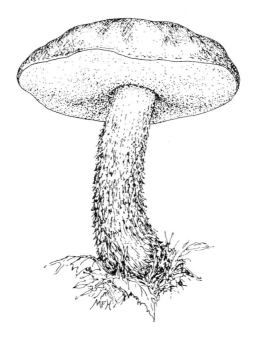

Above: Leccinum scabrum *has a variable cap color, white pores aging to brown and a stem with reddish-brown scabers or scales.*

Leccinum scabrum
▶ **Rough-stemmed Bolete,
Common Scaber Stalk**

The cap is 1.5 to 3 inches broad, variable in color (whitish, reddish or brown) and usually smooth. The flesh is white but darkens when bruised or cut.

The tubes are long but shorter near the stem; whitish when young but brownish when old and sometimes blackish when bruised.

The stem is firm and tapers upward, 2 to 6 inches long and 0.5 to 1 inch thick, whitish but roughened by many reddish or brownish scales.

Spores elliptical, smooth, brown, 15 to 19 x 5 to 7 microns.

COMMON NAME Rough-stemmed Bolete, Common Scaber Stalk

SEASON July–November

EDIBILITY Edible

LOCATION Abundant on the ground in woods

Strobilomyces

Above: Strobilomyces floccopus *is a distinctive mushroom with large grayish-black cottony scales on the cap and stem; the younger white pores darken with age and stain orange-red when bruised.*

This genus, closely resembling Boletus, is represented here by one common species

Strobilomyces floccopus
▶ **Pine Cone Mushroom;**
   Old Man of the Woods

This mushroom is rather common but not abundant. It is edible, however unappealing, and is found growing on the ground in the woods. It will stain quickly when bruised to an orange-red color darkening to black.

The conspicuous, tufted or warty surface of the blackish cap makes this species easily recognizable. The breadth is 2 to 4 inches.

The solid, rough and shaggy, dark stem has a remnant woolly ring or zone left from the partial veil, 3 to 5 inches long, 0.5 to 1 inch thick.

The tubes change with age from whitish to nearly black.

Spores are black with a network of ridges, 9.5 to 15 x 8.5 to 12 microns.

COMMON NAME Pine Cone Mushroom; Old Man of the Woods

SEASON July–October

EDIBILITY Edible

LOCATION Grows in woods

Family

Above: *These brightly colored* Suillus grevillei, *found growing in moss near larch or tamarack trees, have a sticky cap often covered with debris.*

A large group of terrestrial boletes with light-colored pores and smooth stems and spores. Spore prints olive, tan to dark brown.

Suillus grevillei
▶ **Larch Suillus**

A common suillus that is edible after the slimy skin on the cap is removed. A variety,

COMMON NAME Larch Suillus

SEASON September–November

EDIBILITY Edible

LOCATION Moss-covered ground under or near larch trees

Suillus grevillei v. clintonianus, is darker red..

Cap slimy, convex to almost flat, bright yellow to red-brown, 1.5 to 6 inches wide.. Flesh light yellowish-orange bruising pinkish.

Tubes attached or descending the stem, bright yellow, bruising brownish. Medium-sized angular pores.

Stem light yellow with streaks of reddish brown, yellow above the cottony ring with a gelatinous covering, whitish at the base, sticky to slimy. 1.5 to 4 inches long, 0.375 to 1.25 inches wide.

Spores elliptical, smooth, olive-brown, 8 to 10 x 2.5 to 3.5 microns.

Above: *A group of* Suillus luteus, *growing under conifer trees, are commonly known as "Slippery Jack Mushrooms."*

Suillus luteus
▶ **Slippery Jack**

Cap slimy, convex to almost flat, reddish to yellow-brown. Flesh white becoming yellow-ish, 2 to 4.5 inches wide.

Tubes attached, white, pale yellow to olive yellow. Medium-sized angular pores.

Stem covered with brown dots; the veil leaves a purplish-gray sleevelike ring draping the stem. 1.25 to 3.5 inches long, 0.375 to 1 inch wide.

Spores elliptical, smooth, olive-brown, 7 to 9 x 2.5 to 3 microns.

This is a good edible once the slime layer is removed.

COMMON NAME Slippery Jack

SEASON August–December

EDIBILITY Edible

LOCATION Grows in groups or scattered on ground under or near pine or spruce trees

Family

Suillus
Genus

Above: Suillus pictus *is a beautiful mushroom found growing under Eastern white pine late in the summer to early fall.*

Suillus pictus
▶ Painted Suillus

The cap of this handsome, noticeable species, 1 to 3 inches broad, is covered, when mature, with reddish scales, separated from each other by yellowish cracks. Flesh is yellow becoming pinkish.

A veil covers the undersurface of immature caps and sometimes fragments of it remain attached to the margin of the fully developed cap. The pores that are revealed are large, yellow and bruise brownish.

The spores are elliptical, smooth, olive-brown, 8 to 12 x 3.5 to 5 microns.

This beautiful suillus is easily identified and also know as *Suillus spraguei.*

COMMON NAME Painted Boletinus; Painted Suillus

SEASON August–September

EDIBILITY Edible

LOCATION Grows in abundance under Eastern white pine

Clavaria (Coral Mushrooms)

Above: *A specimen of* Clavicorona pyxidata *growing on a moss-covered log has crown-like tips on its branches.*

This genus is now smaller than it was as it has been split into these other genera: *Clavicorona, Clavariadelphus, Clavulina, Clavulinopsis, Ramaria,* and *Ramariopsis.*

These fungi are so named because of their resemblance to branched coral. Some are edible, although some taste bitter and a few are toxic. They may be cooked in the same manner as are gilled and other mushrooms. Each one should be carefully examined before being prepared for the table. If the base is tunneled by larvæ the whole plant must be discarded as it will probably be found to have a bitter taste. The spores are borne on the surface of the branches or plates.

Clavicorona pyxidata
▸ Crown Tipped Coral

This coral fungus was formerly known as *Clavaria pyxidata.* A white to pale yellow coral fungus, somewhat small with many forked branches, crown-shaped at their ends. The branches are 2 to 5 inches in height, and there is a short stalk that is white to pinkish. The spores are white, elliptical and 4 to 5 x 2 to 3 microns in diameter.

COMMON NAME Crown Tipped Coral

SEASON August–October

EDIBILITY Edible

LOCATION On ground on rotting wood

Above: *This* Ramaria Formosa v. concolor *is one of a group of similar pinkish-tan colored coral fungi with many varieties.*

Ramaria formosa v. concolor
▶ Pinkish Coral

This coral is medium to large with many branches arising from a solid base. The color is pale pinkish-beige that turns brown. The flesh is not gelatinous and it is poisonous.

Spores gold to yellow, cylindrical with ridges.

This fungus was formerly called *Clavaria Formosa* and is a group of similar corals with many varieties.

COMMON NAME Pinkish Coral

SEASON July–November

EDIBILITY Poisonous

LOCATION Grows on ground

Clavariadelphus
Genus

Above: Clavariadelphus pistillaris *is a club-shaped fungus that has pale yellow to darker tan colors bruising brown. It is often found in large quantities growing in moss or grass.*

Clavariadelphus pistillaris
▶ **Pestle Shaped Clavaria;
Pestle Shaped Coral**

Although classed with the many-branched corals this mushroom, as its name suggests, is shaped like a club and grows singly or in groups. The rounded, club-like upper end of each stem is puckered, fleshy, white within and spongy. The clubs are from 2 to 10 inches in height. This is an edible mushroom. They vary in color; some are yellow, others are darker in shade, turning brown when bruised.

The elongated, white spores are 10 microns in length and 5 microns broad.

COMMON NAME Pestle Shaped Clavaria; Pestle Shaped Coral

SEASON August–October

EDIBILITY Edible

LOCATION Grow in woods, in mossy or grassy places

Clavariadelphus

Above: *These specimens of* Clavariadelphus truncatus *show the stages of growth from immature to the typical flat-topped mature forms.*

Clavariadelphus truncatus
▶ **Flat Topped Clavaria;**
  Flat Topped Coral

This coral mushroom is shaped like a flattened club and grows singly or in groups. It is an edible mushroom. The club-like upper end of each stem is flattened, fleshy, white within and spongy. The clubs are from 2 to 6 inches in height. They are yellow-ochre to orange darkened with age.

The elliptical, smooth spores leave an ochre print and are 9 to 13 x 5 to 8 microns.

COMMON NAME Flat Topped Clavaria; Flat Topped Coral

SEASON August–October

EDIBILITY Edible

LOCATION Grows on the ground in woods

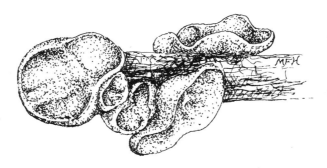

Above: Auricularia auricula *is the common black to brown gelatinous ear-shaped fungus that grows on decaying wood.*

Auricularia auricula
▶ Little Ear, Tree Ear, Ear of Judas

This common gelatinous, almost black mushroom is lobed and folded in a manner suggestive of the form of a human ear. Why it got the name, Ear of Judas is not apparent, except perhaps as explained by Nina L. Marshall in the Mushroom Book (New York, 1903.): "Its habit of growing on elder has given rise to the belief that Judas Iscariot hanged himself on this tree."

They are hairy and yellowish- to reddish-brown beneath and in spite of their dark color the spores are white; 12 to 15 x 4 to 6 microns.

Each fruiting body or cap is from 1 to 4 inches in breadth and is edible.

COMMON NAME Little Ear, Tree Ear, Ear of Judas

SEASON May–December

EDIBILITY Edible

LOCATION On decaying coniferous wood

Family

Calocera
Genus

Above: *This* Calocera viscosa *is an oddly shaped fungus that can be found on coniferous wood from late summer through late fall.*

Calocera viscosa
▶ **Yellow Tuning Fork, Yellow False Coral, Staghorn Jelly Fungus**

This yellow-orange fungus is an inhabitant of coniferous wood. It is gelatinous and coral-shaped with forked tips branching from a rooted white base. It is small; 1 to 4 inches.

The spores are ochre, smooth, sausage-shaped, 9-14 x 3 -5 microns.

It typically grows scattered or in groups.

COMMON NAME Yellow Tuning Fork, Yellow False Coral, Staghorn Jelly Fungus

SEASON August–November

EDIBILITY Unknown

LOCATION On decaying coniferous wood

Above: *This* Tremella mesenterica *is a gelatinous fungi growing on a* Stereum *species of parchment fungus.*

Tremella mesenterica
▶ Witches Butter

Also known as *Tremella lutescens*. This gelatinous fungus is convoluted with lobes and folds, translucent yellow to yellow-orange without a stalk, 0.5 to 2.5 inches wide and up to 1 inch high.

The spores are almost round, smooth, and yellowish; measuring 8 to 12 x 7 to 9 microns in diameter.

It grows on deciduous wood and on other fungi such as various *Stereum* species.

COMMON NAME Witches Butter

SEASON Year-round

EDIBILITY Edible

LOCATION Grows on deciduous wood and on other fungi

Family

Above: *This group of* Tremella reticulata, *found growing on a deciduous log, can become up to six inches wide.*

Tremella reticulata
▶ *White Jelly Fungi*

This gelatinous fungus has hollow lobes and folds, white becoming dingy yellow without a stalk, 2 to 6 inches wide and up to 6 inches high.

The spores are oval, smooth; 9 to 11 x 6 microns in diameter.

COMMON NAME White Jelly Fungi

SEASON July–October

EDIBILITY Unknown

LOCATION Grows on decaying hardwood

Above: *These* Craterellus cornucopioides *are related to* Chanterelles *and can be found among leaf debris in mixed woods.*

Craterellus cornucopioides
▶ **Horn of Plenty; Black Trumpet**

Craterellus is one of the genera that is in the family, *Cantharellaceae,* and it is now grouped with them. This choice edible is almost identical with *Craterellus fallax*, a species so similar it may be a variety. It is also a choice edible.

This brown to almost black, velvety trumpet-shaped mushroom is from 2 to 4 inches in height and half as much in breadth. The edge of the cap is wavy, split, or in folds. The substance is thin but may be either brittle or tough.

The outer or under spore-bearing surface has neither gills, pores nor spines. The spore print is white to pale yellow; the spores are elliptical, smooth; 8 to 11 x 5 to 7 microns.

COMMON NAME Horn of Plenty; Black Trumpet

SEASON July–September

EDIBILITY Choice edible

LOCATION On ground in mixed woods; scattered or in groups

Above: Dentinum repandum *have descending teeth instead of gills or pores and can be found through the summer months.*

These mushrooms are characterized by having teeth or spines pointing downward to afford greater surface on which spores may be formed. They serve the same purpose. as the upright branches of the *Clavarias*.

Dentinum repandum
▶ *Sweet Tooth*

Also known as *Hydnum repandum*. This species resembles a gilled mushroom, having the ordinary cap and stem. Another species, *Dentinum imbricatum*, is somewhat like a smaller version of *D. repandum*, except that its brown upper surface is cracked and scaly and there is a depression in the center of the cap descending through the stem.

The undersurface of the white or buff to brownish-orange cap (1.5 to 5 inches broad) has straight, white brittle teeth beneath, instead of gills.

The stem is 1 to 4 inches long and 0.5 to 1 inches thick. The species is a choice edible, growing on the ground in mixed woods.

The spores are round, smooth, colorless but produce a white spore print; 6 to 8 microns in diameter.

COMMON NAME Sweet Tooth

SEASON July–November

EDIBILITY Choice edible

LOCATION On ground in mixed woods

Above: *A specimen of* Hericium americanum *shows the distinctive tufts of descending spines. It can be bright white to light tan in color*

Hericium americanum
▶ Comb Tooth

This choice edible was known as *Hydnum coralloides*. One of a group of striking fungi, showing up in such contrast against the substrate on which they grow that they can be seen from a distance in the woods. This is one of the most beautiful, growing in pure white tufts on decayed wood. Its graceful branches appear lacy with the myriad fine white spines hanging from them. The divided and subdivided branches all grow from a common stem.

It may grow to a diameter of 10 inches, the teeth being 0.25 to 0.5 an inch long, and is fairly common.

The spores are almost round, colorless but producing a white spore print; 3 to 5 microns in diameter.

COMMON NAME Comb Tooth

SEASON August–October

EDIBILITY Choice edible

LOCATION On decaying deciduous wood

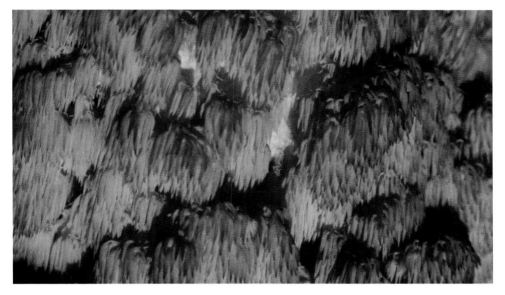

Above: *This group of* Hericium coralloides, *found growing on decaying logs, is a prized edible once the woody debris is removed.*

Hericium coralloides
▶ **Bear's Head Tooth**

This is a handsome white fungus growing on deciduous wood. It has tufts of long, soft teeth hanging like icicles from branches arising from a single stout stem. The whole tufted mass may grow to a diameter of 8 inches, the teeth being half an inch or more long.

Spores almost round; 3 to 5 microns in diameter.

This choice edible was known as *Hydnum caput-ursi* and *Hericium ramosum*.

Somewhat similar to the above is the Satyr's Beard or *Hydnum erinaceum*, but this fungus is usually smaller.

COMMON NAME Bear's head tooth

SEASON July–October

EDIBILITY Edible

LOCATION Grows in a tuft on wood

Hericium erinaceus
▶ **Bearded Tooth**

This is a white fungus growing on deciduous wood. It has spines of soft teeth growing up to 10 inches long growing along its branches arising from a single stout stem.

Spores almost round, colorless but producing a white spore print; 5 to 6 microns in diameter.

This choice edible was known as *Hydnum erinaceum*. It often grows in the same spot each year, usually on damaged beech trees.

Above: *A specimen of* Hericium erinaceus *shows the long tufts of closely-packed spines that are characteristic of this species.*

COMMON NAME Bearded Tooth

SEASON August–November

EDIBILITY Edible

LOCATION Grows in the same spot each year, usually on damaged beech trees

Above: *These tiny* Crucibulum laeve *are in various stages of growth from covered cups to shapes that look like nests of eggs*

Bird's Nest Fungi

The aptly-named bird's nest fungi seldom fail to arouse wonder when first seen, with their little eggs resting in miniature cup-like receptacles. Their spores are contained within the egg-like bodies or *sporangia*, like minute puffballs. There are four families or genera in this order of *nidulariaceae*, namely *cyathus, nidularia, sphaerobolus* and *crucibulum*. They are somewhat alike in gross appearance and size.

COMMON NAME Common Bird's Nest Fungus

SEASON July–November

EDIBILITY Unknown

LOCATION In clusters on decayed wood

All are gastromycetes, that is, "stomach fungi" whose spores are formed on the surface of cells but all enclosed in a pouch or skin.

Crucibulum laeve
▶ Common Bird's Nest Fungus

This fascinating fungus was known as *Crucibulum vulgare.* The commonest species in the genus, it is a tan-colored little bowl, 0.75 to 0.5 inch in diameter, containing several tiny white "eggs" about .0625 in an inch and attached to the nest by a coiled thread. When still immature, these are hidden under a thin, yellowish membrane. Each egg is .

Spores elliptical, colorless; 4 to 10 x 4 to 6 microns.

Calvatia
Genus

Above: Calvatia cyathiformis *has a scaly appearance and a solid white interior that changes to dusty purple spores when mature.*

Puffballs are the safest of all fungi for the beginner to eat, since none, (except for one small species,) are poisonous. If the fungus is smooth and homogenous, white and firm inside, it is a puffball, and fit to be eaten. When cut open, the "egg" or young stage of a deadly *Amanita* shows the embryo stem and cap, and the ball stage of a young stinkhorn shows the stem and a green mass inside, surrounded by a jelly-like substance.

Calvatia cyathiformis
▸ **Pasture Puffball**

Also called Purple-spored Puffball. This globular, whitish-gray or brown fungus, 2 to 6 inches in diameter, springs from a short, thick base on the ground in open fields. Smooth when young; when old it shows a network of cracks. Past its prime, the sac splits and the dry contents are scattered by the wind, leaving a cup-shaped base.

Brownish-purple spores are round, 5 to 7 microns in diameter, with a toothed surface. With the exception of the Giant Puffball, which is the size of a man's head or greater, this puffball is the largest in eastern North America.

COMMON NAME Pasture Puffball

SEASON July–November

EDIBILITY Edible

LOCATION On ground in fields or lawns

Calvatia
Genus

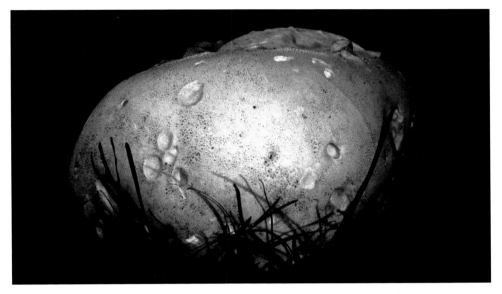

Above: *This* Calvatia gigantea *is the largest member of the puffballs and is found on lawns, open woods or pastures*

Calvatia gigantea
▶ Giant Puffball

The largest of the Puffballs, ranging from 8 to 20 inches, with a white exterior growing from a root-like attachment. It is often found growing singly or in groups in parks, fields, pastures and open woodlands, growing from August to October. The surface is smooth with a tough exterior layer enclosing a white spore mass that gradually turns yellow and then greenish-brown with maturity.

The spores are round, smooth or with tiny warts, greenish-brown, from 3.5 to 5.5 microns.

This is a choice edible when the spore mass is still white throughout. The outer layer sometimes cracks with age. It is also known as *Langermannia gigantea*. There are some regional varieties that have a different texture to the outer skin, but all are edible before the spores change color to yellow or greenish-brown.

COMMON NAME Giant Puffball

SEASON August–October

EDIBILITY Choice edible

LOCATION In parks, fields, pastures, open woodlands; singly or in groups

Lycoperdon perlatum
▸ Gem-studded Puffball

This small puffball was known as *Lycoperdon gemmatum*. It occurs in clusters thickly pressed together, usually growing on the ground but sometimes on dead wood. They are white when young but become gray or grayish brown as they mature. The surface is covered with soft erect scales or warts, and the white flesh turns to black powder as the spores become ready to be expelled through the central opening in the apex at maturity.

The shape of the gemmed puffball is often somewhat like that of a spinning top. It varies in size from 1 to 2.5 inches in height and a little less in breadth.

The brownish spores are about 3 by 4 microns in size.

Like other puffballs, this one is edible when the flesh is still white and firm but the tough skin should be removed and this is not easily done.

Above: *This cluster of* Lycoperdon perlatum *shows the minute soft scales that cover this entire small puffball.*

COMMON NAME Gem-studded Puffball

SEASON July–October

EDIBILITY Edible

LOCATION On ground in open fields or urban areas

Scleroderma citrinum
▶ *Pigskin Poison Puffball*

This puffball is also known as *Scleroderma aurantium*, and was known as *Scleroderma vulgare. Scleroderma citrinum* is poisonous. It is frequently attacked by the Parasitic Bolete, *Boletus parasiticus* (see photograph).

The flesh of this black sheep in the puff-ball family is a slaty or leaden black. Its tough brownish skin is covered with coarse dark scales separated by lighter colored cracks.

This puffball is round or oval and varies in size from 1 to 3 inches in diameter. Unlike some others of the puffballs, this one opens irregularly for spore dispersal and not by a central apical aperture in its skin.

The dingy spores are warty and are 9 to 11 microns in breadth.

Above: *The specimen of* Scleroderma citrinum, *at right, is shown here being .parasitized by* ˮBoletus parasiticus.

COMMON NAME Pigskin Poison Puffball

SEASON July–November

EDIBILITY Poisonous

LOCATION On the ground in woods

Astraeus
Genus

Above: Astraeus hygrometricus *is a small dark gray to brown earthstar that will open its outer segments when wet and close again when dry.*

Geasters or Earth-stars

Geasters or Earth-stars are curiously formed little globes with an outer tough husk which, when mature, separates into pointed fragments, their bases remaining attached to the lower part of the ball or spore-containing sac-like petals of a flower, or a pointed star.

When dry, these segments, seven to 20 in number, fold the ball in their grasp. When wet, they expand or straighten out so as to uncover it again. In some species they bend outwardly and down so far as to rest their tips on the ground and elevate the spore-sac. The spores are discharged through a hole in the top of the sac.

Astraeus hygrometricus
▶ **Water-measuring Earth-star**

This amazing little earth-star will actually open up and stand on its rays when wet, returning to a closed ball when dry. It is the most common species of earth-star and it grows on bare soil.

The outer coat is dark gray and rough, the inner sphere smoother and of a lighter shade. When the pointed segments are unfolded they have a spread of 1.50 to 2 inches. It typically grows from September to November, however it can last over winter without rotting.

The spores are globular, brown and with fine warts on their surface; 7.5-11 microns in diameter.

COMMON NAME Water-measuring Earth-star

SEASON September–November

EDIBILITY Unknown

LOCATION On ground near conifers

Family

Above: *This scattered group of* Geastrum saccatum *are in an advanced stage of maturity growing in an open field.*

Geastrum Saccatum
▶ **Rounded Earth-star**

Another common species that grows in large groups on soil near stumps and dead leaves in mixed woods. The rays are tan to darker brown when mature; the inner spore sac is a lighter shade. When the starlike segments are unfolded they have a spread of 2 or 3 inches. It typically grows from July to October.

The spores are globular, brown and with warts; 3.5 to 4.5 microns in diameter.

This earth-star can last for more months than its growing season, getting darker in color and opening the spore sac to release spores.

COMMON NAME Rounded Earth-star

SEASON July–October

EDIBILITY Unknown

LOCATION Groups on soil near stumps and dead leaves in mixed woods

Ascomycetes or Spore Sac Fungi

The mushrooms described hereinafter differ from all of those mentioned in the preceding pages in the way that their spores are produced. The spores of gilled mushrooms, tube fungi, hedgehog mushrooms (*Hydna* or *Hericium*) coral mushrooms, (*Clavaria* and *Ramaria*) puffballs (*Calvatia, Lycoperdon*), bird's nest fungi (*Nidularia*), are produced on the surface of microscopic cells (*basidia*). These mushrooms are known to botanists as basidiomycetes.

Those described in the following pages, namely, the morels, cup fungi and stinkhorns, produce their minute propagating cells or spores within elongated microscopic sacs (asci), usually in groups of 8, and are known as ascomycetes.

Mutinus caninus
▶ Dog Stinkhorn

An erect hornlike mushroom three or four inches high, usually a little curved in its upper one-fourth, the spore-bearing portion red in color, the stem white to pinkish. It proceeds out of a ragged-edged sheath or cup and is found in woods, bushy places and gardens.

Some of the specimens are odorless but others have a distinctly disagreeable odor which entitles it to be classed as a stinkhorn.

The elliptic smooth spores are 3 to 6 microns long and 2 to 4 microns broad.

McIlvaine is apparently alone in admitting that he has eaten it. He goes so far as to praise its edible quality.

The pinkish stem is more common than the white-stemmed variety known as *Mutinus caninus var. alba.*

Right: *This solitary* Mutinus caninus, *growing in garden soil, has a strong unpleasant scent that attracts flies and will help this stinkhorn to disperse its spores.*

COMMON NAME Dog Stinkhorn

SEASON June–September

EDIBILITY Unknown

LOCATION On ground in woods or gardens

Aleuria
Genus

The Pezizas or cup fungi are ascomycetes, bearing their spores in groups of four or eight in microscopic sacs in their upper or concave surface. They are ordinarily shaped like a cup or saucer and vary in size from that of a pinhead to several inches in breadth. The cup fungi are as a rule leathery in appearance and to the touch and are rarely brittle.

Aleuria aurantia
▶ Orange Peel Cup Fungi

This bright orange cup fungus is 0.75 to 4 inches in breadth and grows on disturbed soil. It is usually sessile but sometimes has a short stem when young.

As it matures the cup spreads out into a saucer shape. It is brittle and the outer surface is pale orange. The growing season is from May to October.

The spores are elliptical with ridges; 18–22 x 9–10 microns.

This common cup fungus is edible and is being studied for medicinal properties.

Right: *Clusters of* Aleuria aurantia *are often found on disturbed ground in large quantities as shown.*

COMMON NAME Orange Peel Cup Fungi

SEASON May–October

EDIBILITY Edible

LOCATION Grows on disturbed soil

Family

Above: *These* Bulgaria inquinans *growing in a cluster on deciduous wood have a gelatinous interior and look like black licorice drops.*

Bulgaria inquinans
▶ Black Jelly Drops

This black cup fungus is 0.375 to 2 inches in breadth and grows on deciduous wood. It is turban-shaped or rounded when young; as it matures the cup becomes flat-topped; it is gelatinous and the outer surface is dull brown and roughened. The growing season is from August to September.

The spores are kidney-shaped, dark brown; 11 to 14 x 6 to 7 microns.

This common cup fungus looks like black licorice drops; its edibility is unknown.

COMMON NAME Black Jelly Drops

SEASON August–September

EDIBILITY Unknown

LOCATION Grows on deciduous wood

Family

Chlorociboria
Genus

Above: *These tiny* Chlorociboria aeruginascens *are cup fungi that have mycelium that stain the wood they inhabit a bright turquoise-green color.*

Chlorociboria aeruginascens
► **Green Stain**

This common cup fungus looks just like someone has painted it along with the wood it inhabits. It is also know as *Chlorosplenium aeruginascens.* Its edibility is unknown.

It is a very small, green cup fungus and rarely seen in its cup form; 0.125 to 0.25 an inch wide. It grows on deciduous wood that becomes stained blue-green with the mycelium threads. The cup often becomes flat.

The growing season is from June to November.

Spores are spindle-shaped, 6 to 10 x 1.5 to 2 microns.

COMMON NAME Green Stain

SEASON June–November

EDIBILITY Unknown

LOCATION Grows on deciduous wood

Disciotus
Genus

Above: Disciotus venosa *are cup fungi that are related to morels and can be found in springtime growing on soil in wooded areas.*

Disciotus venosa
▶ Veined Cup

This reddish-brown cup fungus grows on soil in deciduous woods. It is 2 to 8 inches wide and has a short stem, 0.25 to 0.5 inch long.

As it matures, the cup spreads out into a saucer shape; it has veins or wrinkles on the inner surface and the outer surface is dingy white. The growing season for this fungus is from March to May.

The spores are elliptical and granular, pale yellow; 19 to 25 x 12 to 15 microns.

This common cup fungus is edible with caution and is thought to be related to the Morchellas; like the morels it is poisonous when raw. It is also known as *Discina venosa* or *Peziza venosa*.

COMMON NAME Veined Cup

SEASON March–May

EDIBILITY Edible with caution

LOCATION Grows on soil in deciduous woods

Peziza
Genus

Above: *This group of* Peziza repanda *show the distinctive white outer surface in contrast with the brown interior. The older specimens have split margins.*

Peziza repanda
▶ Recurved Cup Fungi

This pale brown cup fungus 3 to 4 inches in breadth grows on rotten wood or soil and is one of the most conspicuous of the pezizæ. It is usually sessile but sometimes has a short stem when young. As the plant develops the cup spreads out into a saucer shape, its margin sometimes splitting and the color becoming darker. The outer surface is white.

This common cup fungi grows from May to October.

The spores are smooth; 8 to 10 microns broad by 14 to 16 microns long.

Many similar common cup fungus such as *Peziza cerea*, *P. sylvestris* and *P. varia* are also commonly called the recurved cup and the edibility of them is unknown.

COMMON NAME Recurved Cup Fungi

SEASON May–October

EDIBILITY Unknown

LOCATION Grows on rotten wood or soil

Above: *These scarlet* Sarcoscypha coccinea *grow in early springtime on fallen branches of deciduous wood that are sometimes hidden under leaves.*

Sarcoscypha coccinea
▶ Scarlet Cup Fungi

This bright-red cup fungus is 0.75 to 2 inches in breadth and grows on fallen deciduous wood branches. It is usually sessile but sometimes has a short white stem when young. As it matures the cup spreads out into a saucer shape; its outer surface is white. The growing season is from March to June.

The spores are elliptical, smooth; 26 to 40 x 10 to 12 microns.

This beautiful cup fungus looks just like someone spilled bright scarlet red paint on the ground; its edibility is unknown.

COMMON NAME Scarlet Cup Fungi

SEASON March–June

EDIBILITY Unknown

LOCATION Grows on fallen branches of deciduous wood

Wynnea
Genus

Above: *These clusters of the rare fungus,* Wynnea Americana *are shown in their various stages of growth from an underground* sclerotia.

Wynnea Americana
▶ Moose Antlers, Rabbit Ears

This blackish to reddish-brown fungus has branching, elongated, cuplike structures that are antler or rabbit-ear-shaped. They are 1 to 4 inches in breadth, 2.5 to 5 inches tall, and grow on soil in deciduous woods, from an underground mass.

The outer surface is covered with tiny warts, the inner surface is pinkish to reddish brown. The growing season is from July to September.

The spores are elliptical and have a pointed end with longitudinal lines; 32 to 40 x 15 to 16 microns.

This rare fungus seems to have a growth cycle of 11 to 14 years and usually grows only above 1000 feet.

COMMON NAME Moose Antlers, Rabbit Ears

SEASON July–September

EDIBILITY Unknown

LOCATION Grows on soil in deciduous woods

Morels, Morchella
Genus

Above: *These* Morchella elata *have light ridges that darken with maturity resembling pine cones.*
Right: *This solitary* Morchella elata *usually grows a couple weeks earlier than yellow morels. It is found in damp areas often near the edges of paths.*

Morels belong to the botanical family of ascomycetes known as *helvellæ*. The stem and cap are hollow, the cap pitted in a pattern suggesting tripe or honeycomb. Ellipsoid, yellowish spores, about 13 x 22 microns, are borne on the surface of the cap in sacs (asci).

Some morels are poisonous and all cause gastric upset if eaten raw. The only other mushrooms at all resembling morels are false morels, or stinkhorns, which have such an intolerable odor that no one would eat them.

Morchella elata
▸ **Black Morel**

This camouflaged mushroom looks exactly like a pine cone and is hard to see against the ground. It grows April to May in a wide variety of habitats—especially on ground that has been burned over.

1 to 5 inches in height; the conical cap is black, 1 to 2 inches thick, its surface marked by ridges that surround irregular pits, the stem usually white or grayish. Both are hollow with a granular surface that is commonly wrinkled.

A complex species with many different varieties, including *Morchella angusticeps* and *M. conica.*

COMMON NAME Black Morel

SEASON April–May

EDIBILITY Choice edible when cooked

LOCATION Grows on ground that has been burned

Morchella esculenta
▶ **Common Morel, Yellow Morel**

This curious coarse mushroom, its head looking as if covered with tripe, appears in April or May, sometimes as late as June, on ground in sparse woods.

Growing from 2 to 6 inches in height; the somewhat conical cap is from 1 to 2 inches thick and its surface is marked by ridges that surround irregular pits.

The color is tan or brownish, the stem lighter than the head. Cap and stem are hollow, with a granular surface that is commonly wrinkled.

The common morel is prized for its edibility when cooked, but it causes gastric upset when eaten raw.

The most distinctive feature separating it from the false morels is that it is completely hollow with the honeycombed surface joining the stem at the base to the top. False morels have marbled interiors, are more brainlike in looks and are attached at the top of the stem. There are many varieties and different species names, including *Morchella deliciosa* and *M. crassipes*.

Above: *This* Morchella esculenta *close-up shows sunlight passing through the hollow cap and stem.* **Right:** *This specimen of* Morchella esculenta, *found growing at the edge of a lawn, can also be found on disturbed ground in wooded areas.*

COMMON NAME Common Morel, Yellow Morel

SEASON April–May

EDIBILITY Choice edible when cooked

LOCATION Grows on ground in sparse woods

Verpa
Genus

Verpa bohemica
▶ Wrinkled Thimble-cap Morel

Verpa bohemica is also known as *Morchella bispora* or *Ptychoverpa bohemica*. The verpas are edible but it is not recommended, as they are known to cause a lack of muscular coordination if eaten in quantity over a few days.

The lookalikes are *Morchella semilibera* that is a good edible with a partially attached cap, and *Verpa conica* that is also a good edible with a smooth cap attached at the top of the stem.

This mushroom of the morel family grows from March to May on ground in wet wooded areas.

From 2 to 4 inches in height; the wrinkled cap is from 0.5 to 1 inch wide and its surface is attached to the top of the stem only. The color is yellow-brown, the stem is whitish, hollow or stuffed.

Right: *These* Verpa bohemica *can be mistaken for morel sand are not recommended as an edible species.*

COMMON NAME Wrinkled Thimble-cap Morel

SEASON March–May

EDIBILITY Edible but not recommended

LOCATION On ground in wet wooded areas

Family

Gyromitra
Genus

Above: *These specimens of* Gyromitra fastigiata *are known as "False Morels." However, they appear earlier in the spring and are not hollow.*

Akin to the morels, the gyromitras bear their spores in sacs or asci and have stems. Their upper, or spore-bearing surfaces are curiously folded, resembling somewhat the convolutions of the brain. Among the largest of the ascomycetes, the name means twisted bonnet, suggestive of the appearance of these fungi.

Gyromitra fastigiata
▶ Brown Gyromitra

Also called Gabled False Morel, Elephant Ears, or *Gyromitra korfii*. It can cause gastric upset and headaches and is easily confused with *Gyromitra esculenta*, which, while sometimes edible, is reported as cause in a number of poisonings, so it is recommended to avoid it.

A stout, brown, fleshy-stemmed mushroom, the cap 2–4 inches across; contorted into folds. Stem, 1 inch or more thick and 2 inches or more high, solid or spongy and white surfaced; irregular in cross section and seldom cylindrical. On the ground in woods from May to June.

Oval or spherical spores are hyaline, nucleated, 11 microns in diameter or 11 microns by 14 microns when oval.

COMMON NAME Brown Gyromitra

SEASON May–June

EDIBILITY Edible, but not recommended

LOCATION Grows on the ground in woods

Family

Cordyceps
Genus

Above: *This group of* Cordyceps ophioglossoides *have distinctive golden mycelium attaching them to their host.*

Cordyceps ophioglossoides
▶ **Goldenthread Cordyceps**

This mushroom consists of an erect or some-what curved thin stem, 1 to 3 inches in height, with an elongated or spindle-shaped cap a little wider than the stem. The color is reddish brown.

The stem is parasitic on an underground truffle-like fungus species of *Elaphomyces*.

The attachment to the underground host is with gold colored threads of mycelium. The growing season of this uncommon species is August to November.

The spores are partial, elliptical smooth 2.5 to 5 x 2 microns.

There are a few other species of the Genus *Cordyceps*, one of which, *Cordyceps capitata*, is also parasitic on an Elaphomyces species.

Some *Cordyceps* are thought to have medicinal properties, especially in Chinese traditional medicine. This species is of unknown edibility.

COMMON NAME Goldenthread Cordyceps

SEASON August–November

EDIBILITY Unknown

LOCATION Parasitic on underground false truffles

Above: *Clusters of* Leotia lubrica *can be found on damp ground in mixed woods. They have a gelatinous interior and are commonly called "Jelly babies."*

Leotia lubrica
▶ Ochre Jelly Club, Jelly Babies

The Leotias are small gelatinous mushrooms without gills, pores or spines but produce their spores in microscopic sacs (asci), and with their caps and stems they resemble at a distance the gilled mushrooms. *Leotia lubrica* is 1.5 to 2 inches high and 0.5 to 0.75 of an inch broad.

The cap and rather thick stem are hollow when mature.

The whole plant is a dull olive-yellow color. It grows on damp ground in woods, usually in groups from July to October.

The hyaline spores are long and narrow, 22 to 25 microns long and 5 to 6 microns broad. This common species is of unknown edibility.

COMMON NAME Ochre Jelly Club, Jelly Babies

SEASON July–October

EDIBILITY Unknown

LOCATION Grows on damp ground in woods, usually in groups

Family

Above: *These clusters of* Leotia viscosa *show the distinctive green caps.*
Leotia *species are not true jelly fungi despite their common name.*

Leotia viscosa
▸ Green Headed Jelly Club

This species of Leotia is 0.75 to 1.5 inches high and 0.25 to 0.375 of an inch wide. It grows from July to September on soil or rotten wood.

The cap is olive to dark green, the stem is whitish-yellow or orange with tiny green dots. It grows from July to September on damp soil or rotting wood in mixed woods.

The spores are spindle-shaped with round ends, 17 to 26 x 4 to 6 microns.

This common species is of unknown edibility. The Leotias are not true jelly fungi although they resemble them; they have spore sacs (asci) instead of basidia. The similar *Leotia atrovirens* is all green and not as common.

COMMON NAME Green Headed Jelly Club

SEASON July–September

EDIBILITY Unknown

LOCATION Grows on soil or rotten wood

Above: *These* Microglossum rufum *are found growing in damp mossy areas during summer and the early fall seasons.*

Microglossum rufum
▶ **Orange Earth Tongue**

This species is 0.75 to 2.5 inches high and 0.125 to 0.625 inch wide. It grows from July to September on damp soil, rotten wood and among mosses in mixed woods; scattered or in groups.

The cap is yellow-orange and smooth with furrows, the stem is yellow to orange with a granular texture.

The spores are spindle-shaped, smooth; 18 to 40 x 4 to 6 microns.

This common species is of unknown edibility.

COMMON NAME Orange Earth Tongue

SEASON July–September

EDIBILITY Unknown

LOCATION On soil, rotten wood and among mosses, scattered or in groups

Family

Above: *This parasitic* Hypomyces lactifluorum *is a mold that covers its host mushroom, which are usually* Russula *or* Lactarius *species.*

Hypomyces lactifluorum
▶ Lobster Fungus, Lobster Mushroom

This is a bright orange to red mold that parasitizes various species of *Russula* and *Lactarius* mushrooms. The inner flesh remains white. It is found from July to October.

This mold makes a coating of fine bumbs with flasklike vessels over the host species, converting it into a misshapen form often with debris in the depression of the cap.

Spores are spindle-shaped, warted and transparent; 35 to 50 x 4.5 microns.

This can be a common parasite that converts its host into a choice edible, but caution is recommended, as there is a possibility that it can parasitize a poisonous species.

COMMON NAME Lobster Fungus, Lobster Mushroom

SEASON July–October

EDIBILITY Choice edible, with caution

LOCATION Parasitic on Russula or Lactarius species

Lycogala
Genus

Myxomycotina or Slime Molds

The slime molds begin as a gelatinous proto-plasm that can move like amoebas toward a food source. They often appear as one color and shape, only to go through a number of changes, sometimes very quickly, to mature into a completely different form.

They are classified into two major groups: the genus *Ceratiomyxa* that produce their spores externally, and all other slime mold genera that have spore cases in three basic forms. These three forms are: 1.) a spore case on a raised network called a *plasmodiocarp* that is on the edge of the *plasmodium*; 2.) stalked, either alone or in clusters called a *sporangium*; 3.) stalkless, forming a cushion that becomes crustlike and splits to release the spores, called an *aethalium*.

Another distinguishing feature is the presence of sterile threads, called *capillitium*, which mix with the spores in the spore cases.

Lycogala epidendrum
▶ **Wolf's Milk Slime, Toothpaste Slime**

This slime mold begins as a reddish-colored mass, becoming a pink soft larger cushion that exudes pink paste when damaged.

The size is 0.125 to 0.625 in diameter, growing on decaying wood from June to November. The cushions thicken at maturity and turn gray to yellowish brown or black. The paste becomes a darker ochre color and then turns into powdery spores.

Spores are round, netted, light purple to ochre; 6 to 7.5 microns in diameter. The pseudocapillitium is branching, flattened and tubular with transverse folds.

This species is common and can be found in groups. It was known as *Lycoperdon epidendrum*. The lookalike is *Lycogala flavofuscum* which is larger and has a hard outer wall.

Right: Clusters of Lycogala epidendrum *are pink and have a soft paste-like interior changing to grayish-brown on the exterior of their cushion shaped forms.*

COMMON NAME Wolf's Milk Slime, Toothpaste Slime

SEASON June–November

EDIBILITY Unknown

LOCATION Grows on decayed wood

Family

Physarum polycephalum
▶ **Many Headed Slime,
Grape Cluster Slime**

This slime mold begins as a branching, yellowish mass with visible veins. It becomes fan-shaped, producing clusters of rounded granular heads at the edges.

The size is highly variable depending on the moisture of the host wood, other organic debris, or on fleshy fungi. The heads at the edges are 0.0625 to 0.125 inch wide and 0.03125 to 0.24 inch high.

Spores are round, with tiny spines, purple to brown or black in mass; 9 to 11 microns in diameter. The *capillitium* is dense, long, translucent to yellow-to-white with spindle-shaped or irregular nodes.

This species is common and very brightly colored. There is a lookalike named *Physarum cinereum*, which is another common related species.

Above: Physarum polycephalum *is a slime mold that quickly spreads along its host with vein-like structures and fan-shaped granular heads at its leading edge.*

COMMON NAME Many Headed Slime, Grape Cluster Slime

SEASON June–October

EDIBILITY Unknown

LOCATION Grows on leaf debris, rotten wood, or other fungi

Glossary

Abortive imperfect or wanting

Acrid sharp or biting to the tongue

Adnate growing into or fast to; said of gills that are attached broadly to the stem

Adnexed said of gills which are adjacent to the stem but not broadly attached to it

Agaric a mushroom having a fleshy cap, on the under side of which are gills

Alutaceous of the color of tanned leather; brownish-yellow

Annulus the collar or ring on the stem of a mushroom formed by the separation of the veiled

Appressed applied closely to the surface; said of the margin of a cap which lies closely against the stem

Arcuate arched; shaped like a bow

Argillaceous see Clay-colored

Astringent puckery to the taste

Aurantiaceous orange-colored

Basidia mother cells on the spore-bearing surface of agarics and certain other fungi, from which the spores are cast off

Bay a rich dark-reddish chestnut color; badious

Buff a light, dull, brownish yellow, like the color of chamois skin

Bulbous said of the stem of a mushroom when it has bulb-like swelling at the base

Caespitose growing in the tufts or clumps

Campanulate bell-shaped

Cap pileus; the expanded, umbrella-like top portion of a common gilled mushroom

Cartilaginous firm and tough, gristly

Cell (a) a small cavity; (b) a mass of protoplasm, generally microscopic in size; the fundamental form element of every organized body

Centimeter a measure of length; the one-hundredth part of a meter, equal to 0.3937 of an inch

Cinnabarine cinnabar-colored; bright red; vermilion

Clay-colored a dull, light brownish-yellow, intermediate between yellow ochre and Isabelle-color; argillaceous

Close packed closely, side by side; said of gills when they are close together; crowded

Comate hairy

Context texture; substance

Convex elevated and regularly rounded; forming the segment of a sphere or nearly so

Coriaceous of leathery texture

Corrugated puckered; wrinkled

Cortina a web-like veil; the partial veil under the gills of mushrooms of the genus Cortinarius

Cryptogam a plant having an obscure method of fertilization; in botany, in the Linnean system of classification, the great series and final class, including all plants having no stamens and pistils, and therefore no proper flowers

Cyathiform cup-shaped

Decurrent said of gills which extend down the stem of a mushroom

Deliquescent said of mushrooms that liquefy or melt when old

Dichotomous dividing in two; said of gills that are regularly forked

Dimidiate said of gills that extend half way from the edge of the cap to the stem, also of caps that are more or less semicircular in outline

Disc the central portion of the upper surface of a mushroom's cap

Distant said of gills that are far apart

Eccentric away from the center; between the center and the edge of a cap

Elliptical parallel-sided and rounded at the ends

Emarginate notched at the end; said of gills whose lower edge is scooped out at a point near the inner end

Epidermis the peel or skin

Farinaceous mealy; brain-like; said of taste or odor

Fibrous provided with fibers

Flesh the inner substance of the cap or body of a fungus

Flesh-color a color like that of healthy human skin

Floccose downy; woolly; flaky

Free said of gills that do not reach the stem

Fulvous a yellowish-brown tint like that of tanned leather, tawny

Fungus a cryptogamous plant characterized by absence of chlorophyll and getting its nourishment from organic matter

Gelatinous jelly-like

Genus a group of species that posses characteristics in common

Gills the plates attached to the lower surface of an agaric, and on which the spores are formed

Glabrous smooth; without down or hairs

Glaucous dull-green, passing to grayish-blue

Globular globose, nearly spherical

Gregarious in groups (not tufts)

Habitat natural abode

Hyaline transparent; clear, like glass

Hygrophanous of a water-soaked appearance when moist but opaque when dry

Hymenium the spore-bearing surface covering each side of the gills of a mushroom

Hymenomycetes mushrooms that have an exposed spore bearing surface and in which the spores are borne on basidia

Hymenophore the under surface of the cap, to which the gills are attached

Hypha (pl. **hyphae**), a cylindrical thread of the mycelium. Branched threads from the spawn from which mushrooms grow

Infundibuliform funnel-shaped

Isabelline a light buff-brown color

Involute rolled inwards

Laccate appearing as if lacquered or varnished

Lamella a gill

Leucosporae a group of mushrooms having white spores

Lignatile growing on wood

Lobed having rounded divisions

Micron a unit of measure; the one-thousandth part of a millimeter; 0.000039 inch. To convert microns to inches, multiply them by (approximately) 0.00004

Mold, Mould (1) fine, soft earth rich in organic matter; (2) a kind of minute fungus

Mushroom a cryptogamic plant of the class fungi; applied in a general sense to almost any of the larger conspicuous fungi, such as toadstools, puff balls, hydnei, etc., but more particularly to the agaricoid fungi and especially to the edible forms

Mycelium the spawn of fungi; rootlike threads resulting from the germination of spores, from the masses of which the mushroom arises

Mycology the science of fungi

Mycophagist one who eats fungi

Ochraceous color of ochre, a natural earth element used as pigment, commonly understood to mean the color of iron-rust

Olivaceous a greenish-brown color like that of olives

Pallid pale, deficient in color

Papilionaceous resembling the butterfly; mottles as the gills of some species of Panaeolus that are mottled with black spots

Parasite a plant growing on or in another living body from which it derives nourishment **Partial** said of a veil that surrounds the stem of a mushroom and extends to the edge of the cap

Peronate said of the stem of a mushroom when it has a boot-like or stocking-like covering

Personate masked or disguised

Pileus cap; the head of a mushroom

Porphyrosporae a group of mushrooms that have purple or purplish-brown spores

Pruinate covered with a frost-like bloom

Radiate, Radiating arranged like the spokes of a wheel

Resupinate said of a mushroom that is attached to the wood on which it grows by its back and without a stem

Revolute turned upwards or backwards; the opposite of involute

Rhodosporae a group of mushrooms that have pink or rosy spores

Rimose cracked

Ring a part of the partial veil adhering to the stem of a mushroom like a collar, annulus

Rubescent blushing; reddish

Rufus a brownish-red color

Sapid savory; agreeable to the taste

Separable capable of being detached

Sessile seated; attached by the base and without a stem

Sinuate waved; said of the edge of gills that are notched near the stem

Species an individual or individuals that differ from all other members of a genus and that propagate others of their own kind

Spore a minute cell that is the reproductive body of cryptogams

Squamose scaly; scale-like

Stipe stem of a mushroom

Striate having a parallel or radiating lines or furrows

Sub as a prefix signifies slightly, almost or somewhat

Tawny color of tanned leather

Toadstool any umbrella-shaped fungus. The name is usually restricted to gilled fungi but is also applied to almost any fungus that is large enough to attract general attention such as boleti, hydnei, morel, etc. Popularly, the name *toadstool* is applied only to those fungi that are supposed to be poisonous, as distinguished from mushrooms or edible forms. As a matter of fact all true toadstools are really mushrooms, and may or may not be poisonous.

Tomentose covered with dense wool or hair

Umbilicate provided with a pit or central depression; having a navel-like depression at the center

Umbo the central elevation or knob of some mushrooms

Umbonate with a central knob or boss-like elevation

Universal veil the outer wrapper or membrane (volva) which envelops a mushroom in its youngest stage

Vaginate contained within a sheath or volva

Veil a covering or membrane enveloping a fungus, occurring chiefly among the agarics. See partial veil and universal veil

Veins swollen wrinkles on the sides of gills and on the under surface of a cap of a mushroom between the gills, often connected and forming cross partitions

Villose downy; with soft hairs

Viscid moist and sticky; glutinous

Volva the universal veil (q.v.); sometimes applied to that portion remaining in the form of warts on the surface of the cap (as in Amanita muscaria) or in the form of a cap at the base of the stem

Wart a scale on the surface of the cap of a mushroom, the remains of the volva

Zones circular zones of color on the surface of the cap of a mushroom, as seen in Lactarius deliciosus

Index

MUSHROOM FORAY LIST

Species	Location	Observations

MUSHROOM FORAY LIST

Species	Location	Observations

MUSHROOM FORAY LIST

Species	Location	Observations